DELICIOUS
NUTRITIOUS
AND SIMPLE

Delicious, Nutritious, and Simple:
Super High-Nutrient Recipes for Health and Healing

Copyright © 2015 Dale Figtree

www.dalefigtree.com

ISBN-13:978-1505782745
ISBN-10:1505782740

Special thanks to Margaret Dodd and Ilene Segalove for their skillful and creative input.

Artwork by Dale Figtree

Designed by Margaret Dodd, Studio K Communication Arts
studiokarts@earthlink.net

www.createspace.com

CONTENTS

A High-Nutrient Way of Eating

Delicious, Nutritious, and Simple is a collection of tasty, tried-and-true, high-nutrient recipes that provide your body with abundant quantities of vitamins, minerals, water, fiber, healthy fats, balanced proteins, and quality carbohydrates. Why choose high-nutrient food? Great fuel powers great performance for all the cells of your body — all 75 billion of them! In today's world, where food is often depleted of so many essential nutrients, *Delicious, Nutritious, and Simple* is designed to maximize your health and well-being and help you choose and prepare easy-to-digest, easy-to-make, satisfying and flavorful meals.

As a seasoned nutritionist, I am passionate about introducing you to this new level of eating based on nutrient-dense recipes that go beyond the basics of consuming food to just get through the day. That "beyond" translates into extra raw materials and energy to support the deepest and most potent healing and regenerative work the body is capable of providing.

With intensive nutritional support, I have not only witnessed my own healing from lymphatic cancer, but have also witnessed profound healing in many of my clients of degenerative diseases, from diabetes to heart disease. Degenerative disease is not usually caused by bacteria or viruses, but by the slow degeneration of tissue in different organs of the body. To a great degree, this is influenced by comsuming too many clogging, irritating, depleting or chemical-laden foods, and not enough high-nutrient foods to support the body's extraordinary cleansing and healing ability.

Since food is the main focus of my work, when it comes to my own food, I want simple — simple to prepare, and simple to digest! Over the years I have created and collected an array of high-nutrient, easy-to-make recipes, which in turn I pass on to my clients,

DELICIOUS, NUTRITIOUS AND SIMPLE

who also appreciate their simplicity as well as their flavor. Finally I have compiled these special recipes into a book — recipes that fit into the health-supporting food programs that I so strongly advocate.

It is a pleasure to bring these life-enhancing meals into your life and onto your dining table. May you enjoy and benefit from the recipes in *Delicious, Nutritious, and Simple*, and may this book bring you health and happiness.

Dale Figtree, PhD

Breakfast

Breakfast means "break the fast." After not eating for 6 to 8 hours, our nutrient reserves are low and need to be replenished. That is where a high-nutrient meal can make the greatest difference — in establishing a strong foundation for the day, and in assuring our metabolism there are plentiful nutrients available to go full speed ahead in our energy output. Plentiful nutrients means choosing high-nutrient foods that include a good variety of vitamin and mineral-rich carbohydrates, protein, and healthful fats. The following recipes supply all of these rich nutrients.

To start your morning in the most potent health-supporting way, I suggest beginning breakfast with a freshly made vegetable juice (page 107). These juices amp up nutrient intake to levels that would be difficult to reach by only eating whole foods.

All breakfast recipes are for one person, unless otherwise indicated.

All nuts listed in these recipes are meant to be raw and unsalted, or soaked and dehydrated at low temperature to preserve healthy fats.

Fresh Fruit Ambrosia with Chopped Nut Topping

1 lb fruit, cut into bite-size pieces
1 oz walnuts, pecans or almonds
   plus one or all of the following:
1 celery stalk, chopped finely or a
   handful of chopped sunflower sprouts
Optional: 1 tbsp dried coconut flakes

1. Mix together fruit with the chopped greens.
2. Chop or grind nuts in blender. Sprinkle on top of fruit salad and toss.
3. Mix into fruit salad, coating all the fruit.

Optional: Instead of nuts, try 2 heaping tbsp of sesame butter thinned with carrot juice or water.

Instant Chia Porridge
(grain-free)

2 1/2 tbsp chia seeds
1 cup hot water
1 cup berries or 1 pear, or 1 apple, chopped
1 tbsp unsweetened, grated coconut
3 tbsp hemp seeds

1. Pour hot water into serving bowl, add chia seeds, and stir for 1 minute.
2. Add the rest of the ingredients and stir again until thick.

DELICIOUS, NUTRITIOUS AND SIMPLE

Breakfast Gazpacho

This is the most nutrient-dense breakfast of all. For people wanting to push their nutrient base higher, this is the way to go.

1 tomato
1/2 red bell pepper
1/2 apple
1/2 cucumber
1/2 lemon, peeled and seeded
4 leaves romaine lettuce
1 celery stalk

1. Cut up all ingredients (except celery stalk).
2. Blend in food processor or blender (in blender push down mixture with celery stalk or carrot) and serve immediately.
3. For a complete balanced meal, follow with 1 to 2 fruits and 1 oz raw, unsalted almonds or other raw nuts or seeds.

Millet Waffles

Serves 4

2 cups millet
2 tbsp olive oil
2 tbsp maple syrup
1/2 tsp salt
1/2 tsp ground coriander
water
Topping: cinnamon, berries

1. Wash millet and put in large bowl with 1 1/2 cups water and soak overnight.
2. Drain and rinse millet. Put in blender with 1 cup water and the remaining ingredients and blend to a thick batter.
3. Put some batter onto a hot waffle iron, close and bake. Repeat with remaining batter.
4. Dust with cinnamon and serve with fresh berries on top.

Buckwheat Powerhouse

Buckwheat supports longer-lasting energy, more so than any other grain cereal I've ever tried! And it is good-tasting, too!

1/2 cup raw or toasted buckwheat groats
1 1/2 cups water
1/4 small onion, chopped
1/2 zucchini, chopped
1/2 carrot, chopped
Garnish: 1/2 ripe avocado, chopped

DELICIOUS, NUTRITIOUS AND SIMPLE

1. Bring water to boil and add buckwheat and all other ingredients.
2. Reduce heat to simmer, cover and cook until all water is absorbed, usually about 12 minutes.
3. Garnish with avocado and serve.

Stewed Fruit Sprinkled with Chopped Walnuts

1 apple, peeled, seeded, and cut into small pieces
4 dried pears
4 dried apricots
4 dried prunes
10 raisins
1/2 tsp Pumpkin Pie Spice*
1 cup water
1 oz walnuts, finely chopped

1. Soak all dried fruit overnight in 1 cup of water.
2. In morning, put water and soaked fruit in a pot with chopped apple. Add Pumpkin Pie Spice and mix.
3. Bring to a boil, then simmer for 3 minutes.
4. Pour fruit, chopped celery, and liquid into serving bowl.
5. Sprinkle walnuts on top, toss and serve.

Available in most stores

Crunchy Maple Nut Granola
(oil free, grain-free)

This recipe yields a large quantity of granola that can be made in advance and stored. It is the most delicious granola I have ever tasted. Its nutritional content is greatest if it is made in a dehydrator (as the low temperature of 110°F will not destroy the omega-3 oils in the nuts). If you do not have a dehydrator, it can also be made in an oven set to the lowest temperature. You may sacrifice some of the good oils, but it is still a very healthful breakfast, high in protein, fiber, vitamins and minerals. Takes a lot of prep and work to make, but it is worth it!

3 cups almonds
3 cups walnuts
3 cups whole cashews
3 cups sunflower seeds
2 cups pumpkin seeds
1 1/2 cups sesame seeds
1 cup pure maple syrup (Grade B)
1 cup fresh apple juice
2 tsp vanilla extract
1 1/2 tsp salt
2 tbsp cinnamon
1 tsp Pumpkin Pie Spice*

1. In a food processor, lightly grind almonds, cashews and walnuts to desired texture (keeping the nuts chunky). Transfer to a large bowl.
2. Add whole pumpkin and sunflower seeds, salt, and dry spices to the bowl.
3. Mix maple syrup, apple juice, and vanilla. Pour over nut mixture and mix well by hand to coat everything.

* Available in most stores

DELICIOUS, NUTRITIOUS AND SIMPLE

4. Sprinkle in the sesame seeds, and mix well again.
5. Spread 4 cups per sheet on parchment paper-lined dehydrator trays.
6. Dehydrate at 110°F for 12 hours or until dried and crisp.
7. Crumble each sheet into loose granola and store in airtight containers.
8. Serve with fresh fruit and almond/brazil nut milk.

Courtesy of Dianne Bess

Cinnamon Oatmeal Cooked with Fruit and Nuts

1/2 cup natural rolled oats* (not instant)
1 apple, chopped, or 1/2 cup blueberries, or sliced banana
1/4 tsp cinnamon
1 1/2 cups water
1/4 cup walnuts or almonds, chopped

* Steel cut or oat groats are even more nutritious but require extra cooking time.

1. Boil water and add oats. Cover and simmer for 5 minutes.
2. Add fruit and continue cooking for another 3 minutes.
3. In a serving bowl, sprinkle finely chopped nuts on top.

The oatmeal should be creamy and not need any other liquid, but unsweetened almond milk may be added if desired.

Creamy Polenta Cooked with Fruit and Nuts

1/2 cup dried polenta
1 chopped fruit, or 1/2 cup berries,
   or 3/4 cup dried fruit soaked overnight
2 1/2 cups water
1/4 cup walnuts or almonds, finely chopped

1. Boil water, then reduce heat to medium. Slowly stir in the polenta, mixing continuously for about 2 minutes until completely dissolved.
2. Mix in fruit, cover and simmer about 3 more minutes until creamy. Add water if too thick.
3. Pour mixture into a serving bowl and sprinkle finely chopped nuts on top.

Banana Walnut Pancakes

2 large eggs (hormone-free and free-range)
1 banana, ripe (brown spots on skin)
1/2 tsp cinnamon
1/4 cup walnuts
olive oil as needed

1. Grind walnuts until fine. Use a spatula to separate from sides of blender.
2. Add to blender remaining ingredients and blend again until smooth.
3. In a cast-iron frying pan, heat enough olive oil to coat the bottom in a thin layer. When the oil is hot, turn down heat to medium-low

DELICIOUS, NUTRITIOUS AND SIMPLE

and pour some of the mixture into pan with a ladle, forming 2- to 3-inch pancakes.

4. When little bubbles begin to form on top of pancake, flip over and brown other side. Serve immediately.

This recipe is my favorite treat. It is also delicious when an apple is substituted for a banana.

Eggs Florentine

2 large eggs
1/2 small onion, chopped
1/4 red bell pepper, chopped
1 small zucchini, chopped
handful of spinach or a chard leaf, chopped
sesame seeds, ground, or Gomasio*
   (ground sesame seeds with salt)
1 tbsp olive oil

1. Coat a cast-iron frying pan with olive oil and immediately add 1/4 inch of water and heat to boiling.
2. Turn down heat to a low boil and add chopped vegetables. Cover with lid and cook for 3 minutes.
3. Break open 2 eggs over mixture, cover and cook another 3 minutes.
4. Sprinkle with ground sesame seeds or Gomasio and scoop out with spatula and serve.

* Available in most health food stores

Note about Teflon-coated pans

Originally I made this recipe in a Teflon-coated pan without using oil. However, information has recently surfaced about the long-term toxic effects of using Teflon and other stick-free coated pans, so I now prefer cast iron. As some bird owners will know, if the heat gets high enough on Teflon, the resultant fumes can actually kill their pet. Studies suggest those fumes may contain some level of toxicity for humans as well.

Almond French Toast

Serves 2

> 4 slices Almond Bread (page 92)
> 2 eggs, beaten
> 1/4 tsp cinnamon
> olive oil
> 1 apple, chopped coarsely, or 8 strawberries, sliced

1. Mix the eggs and cinnamon in a shallow dish.
2. Coat both sides of each slice of almond bread with egg mixture.
3. In cast-iron fry pan, coat bottom thinly with olive oil and heat.
4. Grill slices of almond bread on each side until slightly brown.
5. At the same time, add chopped fruit to the pan and grill lightly.
6. Serve with fruit on top.

DELICIOUS, NUTRITIOUS AND SIMPLE

Scrambled Veggie/Tofu

Serves 4

> 1 lb firm tofu
> 1 tbsp tamari sauce
> 1/4 tsp curry powder or turmeric
> handful of shitake mushrooms, sliced
> 1 zucchini, diced
> 1 red bell pepper, diced
> 1/2 onion, diced
> olive oil
> *Optional: black pepper*

1. Mash tofu in bowl.
2. Add tamari sauce and curry and pepper. Mix well and set aside.
3. Heat a little olive oil in frying pan and add onion, red bell pepper, mushrooms and zucchini, and stir for a few minutes until onions become transparent.
4. Add tofu and stir well. Sauté for another 5 minutes and serve.

Courtesy of Beatrix Rohlsen

Salads

Salads are among the healthiest foods you can eat. Because they are raw, their strong nutrient levels are intact. They are composed of energy-supportive carbohydrates and provide high amounts of vitamins, minerals, fiber, and the best water money can buy. Of course the dressing put on the salad can make or break its health-supporting qualities, but by adding a dressing that contains cold-pressed olive oil, you are increasing the balance of healthful fats in what is already a powerful brew of nutrients.

Most salad recipes are for 2 to 4 portions, unless otherwise noted.

Tossed Salad for One

3 to 4 leaves of romaine or other red or green lettuce (except iceberg), cut into bite-size pieces

6 cherry tomatoes, sliced in half, or 1 tomato, chopped

1/2 red bell pepper, chopped (higher in vitamin C than the green variety)

1/2 cucumber (peeled, if waxed), chopped

1 carrot, grated

1 celery stalk, chopped

Optional: chopped red onion or scallions, handful of sunflower or daikon radish sprouts, kalamata olives (pitted and chopped), grated radish, red cabbage, or any other additional raw vegetables

1. Mix all ingredients together.
2. Toss with Lemon Herb Dressing (page 35) or other healthful dressing of your choice.

Can add or follow with 1 chopped fruit, plus 2 to 4 oz chopped raw nuts to make a complete meal.

Greek Salad

2 ripe tomatoes, coarsely chopped

1/2 red bell pepper, coarsely chopped

1 cucumber, coarsely chopped

1/2 small red onion, chopped

8 black kalamata olives, pitted and chopped

3 to 4 oz of goat or sheep feta cheese

sprinkle of olive oil

1/2 lemon, juiced

1/4 tsp dried oregano

DELICIOUS, NUTRITIOUS AND SIMPLE

1. Mix together all salad ingredients in a large bowl.
2. Sprinkle with olive oil and lemon juice.

Avocado Gazpacho

This salad is not only super high in nutrients, but it is pre-digested, meaning less energy is used breaking it down in the body, and therefore more energy is conserved.

1/4 to 1/2 avocado
1 tomato
1/2 red bell pepper
1/2 cucumber
1/2 lemon, juiced
4 leaves romaine lettuce
1 celery stalk
Optional: 1/4 red onion, small handful of cilantro or parsley

1. Cut up all ingredients in large chunks (except celery stalk).
2. Blend in food processor or blender (in blender, push down mixture with celery stalk) and serve immediately.

For a complete super high-nutrient meal, follow with 2 or 3 fruits and 2 to 4 oz raw, unsalted nuts or seeds.

To make it spicier, blend with garlic clove, 1 tbsp olive oil, 1 tbsp tamari sauce, and a dash of cayenne pepper.

Spinach/Arugula Salad

2 cups baby spinach leaves, coarsely chopped
1 cup arugula leaves, coarsely chopped
handful of cherry tomatoes, sliced in half
1/2 red onion, chopped
1/2 red bell pepper, chopped
handful of kalamata olives, pitted and chopped
Optional: 2 oz crumbled sheep or goat feta cheese

1. Mix all ingredients together.
2. Sprinkle with Lemon/Herb Dressing (page 35).

Crunchy Fennel Salad

1 medium-sized fennel bulb, sliced once down
    the middle and then very thinly crosswise
1 cup shelled edamame (can be frozen)
2 lemons
3/4 cup fresh mint leaves, sliced in thin ribbons
1/2 cup almonds, chopped
salt and pepper to taste
olive oil
Optional: 1/2 red onion, sliced

1. Cook edamame in a pot of boiling salted water for
    about 5 minutes, then drain.
2. Use a vegetable peeler to peel both lemons, and
    slice the peel in narrow julienne strips.
3. Slice the fennel, place in large bowl and toss with
    juice of one of the lemons to prevent oxidation.

4. Mix in lemon peel, sprinkle with salt to tenderize slightly and add still-warm edamame to bowl. Add 2 tbsp of olive oil, toss to coat.
5. Add more salt, pepper, and lemon juice to taste.
6. Toss mint leaves into salad.
7. Chill salad for a couple of hours to tenderize the fennel.
8. Add chopped almonds just before serving, so they'll stay crisp.

Can be served cold or at room temperature.

Courtesy of Shelley Gault

Coleslaw Salad

4 cups white cabbage, shredded
2 celery stalks, finely chopped
1 small sweet apple, finely chopped
1 large carrot, grated
2 tbsp walnuts, coarsely chopped

1. Mix together all ingredients in a large bowl.
2. Serve with Mustard/Olive Oil Dressing (page 36).

Oriental Salad

1/2 cabbage, shredded
1/2 cup carrot, grated
2 celery stalks, chopped
1/2 red onion, chopped
1 cup bean sprouts
1 chopped scallion

1. Mix together ingredients.
2. Sprinkle with toasted sesame oil and umeboshi plum vinegar or Tahini Dressing/Sauce (page 35).

Seaweed Salad
(highest source of calcium and iodine)

Serves 8

hiziki   red seaweed

arame   dried kelp (fine)

wakame (use very small amount as it swells)

natural strands of agar, cut in one-inch pieces
  and separated

Optional: any other edible dried seaweed you can find

1 scallion, chopped

1/2 cucumber, finely chopped

1. Place a small handful of each of the dried seaweeds in a large bowl, rinse twice, and then let sit covered with water for 20 minutes.
2. Rinse again and store covered with water in glass container.
3. When ready to serve, scoop a handful of seaweed mixture into a colander. Rinse, drain and place in a small dish with cucumber and scallions. Can also be served on a bed of arugula or baby spinach.
4. Sprinkle with toasted sesame seed oil, umeboshi plum vinegar and ground-up toasted sesame seeds.

The cleanest healthiest seaweed is from Maine. This recipe makes a large quantity that can be stored in the refrigerator for up to two weeks, and a little eaten each day.

DELICIOUS, NUTRITIOUS AND SIMPLE

Veggie/Taco Boats

Serves 2

4 leaves red cabbage or savoy cabbage
1/2 carrot, shredded
sprouts
1/2 avocado, sliced or mashed
1 tomato, chopped
2 slices red onion, chopped
2 tbsp chopped cilantro or basil
8 kalamata olives, chopped
1/2 cup walnuts
1/2 tbsp tamari sauce
1/8 tsp cumin

1. In food processor or blender, chop walnuts finely, then add tamari sauce and cumin and blend again.
2. In center of cabbage leaf, place 3 tbsp of nut mixture, then add a heaping tbsp of mashed avocado. Add chopped veggie mixture and top with sprouts.
3. Squeeze together top of leaf and eat like a taco. Serve with napkins handy!

Courtesy of Diane Best

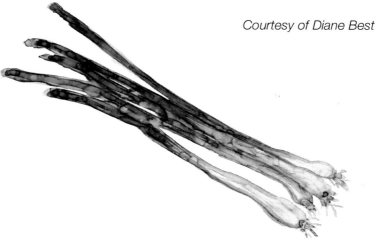

Mixed Bean Salad

Serves 2

> 2 cups beans, cooked (1/3 of each: kidney, black, azuki)
> 1 red onion, diced
> 1 large tomato, diced
> 1/4 cup cilantro, chopped
> 1 cup corn kernels, cooked

1. In a large bowl mix all ingredients together.
2. Toss with Basic Olive Oil Dressing (page 34).

Zucchini Carpaccio Salad with Avocado

> 1 tbsp lemon juice, freshly squeezed
> 1/2 tsp sea salt
> 1/4 cup olive oil
> 4 small zucchini, ends trimmed
> 1/4 cup pistachio nuts, chopped
> 4 sprigs fresh lemon thyme

1. Stir together lemon juice and 1/2 tsp salt in a small jar. Add olive oil, cover and shake to blend.
2. Slice zucchini lengthwise as thin as possible using a mandoline or very sharp knife.
3. Spread slices on a platter and drizzle with lemon mix.
4. Cover with plastic wrap and marinate at room temperature for 30 minutes to 1 hour.

DELICIOUS, NUTRITIOUS AND SIMPLE

5. Alternate zucchini and avocado slices on individual salad plates, slightly overlapping each slice.
6. Sprinkle with pistachio nuts. Season with a little more salt and garnish with lemon thyme.

Courtesy of Linda S. Kelly

Raw Kale Salad with Tahini Sauce

Serves 4 to 6

1 bunch kale, carefully rinsed
1 lemon or lime, juiced
1/2 tsp sea salt
6 tbsp Tahini Dressing/Sauce (page 35)

1. Cut or tear kale from stems into large bite-size pieces.
2. Add lemon or lime juice and sea salt. Toss.
3. Massage kale for 5 minutes (squeeze and release repeatedly).
4. Let sit for at least 15 minutes, then toss with Tahini Dressing/Sauce (page 35).

Dressing alternatives can also combine toasted sesame seed oil and umeboshi plum vinegar with ground sesame seeds on top.

This salad can also be used as a wonderful base for a mixed veggie salad.

Mixed Leaf Herb Salad
with Flowers

1/2 cup mixed fresh herbs, such as chervil, dill, basil, parsley, mint, sorrel, fennel and cilantro (also, but more sparingly, tarragon and marjoram)

A bowlful of mixed salad greens, such as arugula, radicchio, watercress, curly endive, baby spinach, oak leaf, nasturtium (including the flower), plus dandelion greens, and any other edible flowers

1/8 cup olive oil

1 tsp cider vinegar

1 tsp tamari sauce

black pepper

1. Wash and dry herbs and salad leaves.
2. In small bowl blend together olive oil, cider vinegar, tamari sauce, and black pepper to taste.
3. Combine leaves and herbs, pour over dressing and mix well.

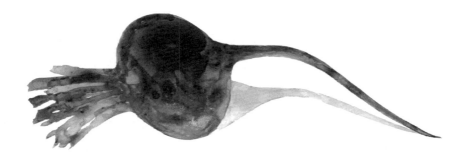

DELICIOUS, NUTRITIOUS AND SIMPLE

Hummus Caesar Salad

4 leaves romaine lettuce, chopped into bite-size pieces
1/2 red bell pepper, finely chopped
1 persian cucumber, finely chopped
small chunk of red onion, finely chopped
1 cup hummus
juice of 1/2 lemon
1 oz water

1. Mix salad ingredients together.
2. Thin hummus with lemon and water.
3. Pour over salad and mix well until all lettuce is coated.

Instead of hummus, guacamole made from a whole avocado can be used.

Red Apple/Beet Salad

1/2 cup raw almonds, slivered or chopped
2 red apples, diced
1/2 lemon, juiced
4 cups mixture of red salad leaves
1 large beet, cooked and sliced
3 tbsp olive oil
1 tbsp apple cider vinegar

1. Toast almonds in dry frying pan for 2 to 3 minutes until golden, tossing frequently.
2. Cover diced apples with lemon juice, then mix with the rest of salad ingredients, add almonds, then toss with oil and apple cider vinegar.

Dressings & Sauces

Dressings are an excellent opportunity to add a greater balance of nutrients to the salad. Extra-virgin olive oil should be the oil of choice, since it is more stable than other oils and unsaturated (not sticky in the blood) at the same time. It should always be cold-pressed and stored in dark glass so it retains its vitamin E and other fine nutrients.

Dressings and sauces can change the taste of a salad or vegetable, especially with strong-tasting herbs like basil, but on the other hand it can also bring out the natural flavors. Oil on vegetables dissolves some of the flavor molecules, making them more available to taste. And lemon brings out the natural saltiness and intensifies other flavors. Salad dressings can be stored in an airtight glass container in a dark cool cabinet.

Make sure your oil is 100% olive oil, as sometimes other oils are added without listing them.

Basic Olive Oil Dressing

1 cup olive oil
1 tbsp tamari sauce or salt to taste
1 garlic clove, crushed
1/2 cup water
juice of 1 lemon, or 2 tbsp balsamic or umbushi plum vinegar

1. Put all ingredients in blender.
2. Blend until smooth.
3. Pour into glass jar to save. Use 1 or 2 tbsp per salad.

Do not refrigerate, but keep in a dark cool cabinet.
Olive oil–based dressings should stay fresh for a week.

Creamy Avocado Dressing

1 medium avocado
1 tbsp lemon juice
1 tbsp red onion, minced
1 tsp tamari sauce
3 tbsp water
1 clove garlic, crushed

1. Put all ingredients in blender.
2. Blend until smooth.
3. Add more water if dressing is too thick.
   Use immediately.

DELICIOUS, NUTRITIOUS AND SIMPLE

Lemon/Herb Dressing

1 cup olive oil
juice of 1 lemon
1 garlic clove, crushed
1/2 cup water
pinch of black pepper, dash of salt
small bunch of freshly chopped
  (or 1/2 tsp dried) oregano, dill or basil
Optional: 1 tsp organic white or yellow miso paste

1. Put all ingredients in blender and blend until smooth.
2. Pour into jar to save. Use 1 or 2 tbsp per salad.

Do not refrigerate, but keep in a dark cool cabinet.

Tahini Dressing/Sauce

1 cup tahini (sesame butter)
juice of 1/2 lemon
1 garlic clove, crushed
1 tbsp tamari sauce
1 tsp toasted sesame oil
water to thin

1. Squeeze lemon juice into tahini, add tamari sauce and garlic clove and mix in blender.
2. Slowly add a little water until consistency of tahini becomes more liquid and pourable, but not too thin.

Keep in refrigerator.

Mustard/Olive Oil Dressing

3 tbsp olive oil
1 spring onion, finely chopped
1/2 tsp powdered or 1 tsp prepared mustard
1 tbsp lemon juice
1 tbsp water
1 tsp tamari sauce

Shake all ingredients in a tightly closed jar or mix in blender.

Artichoke Dipping Sauce

1/2 cup olive oil
1 garlic clove, crushed
juice of 1/2 lemon
1 tbsp tamari sauce
1/4 cup water

Mix in blender and serve with steamed artichokes (page 70).

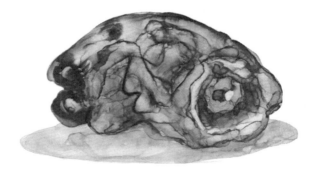

DELICIOUS, NUTRITIOUS AND SIMPLE

Almond Mayonnaise
(Egg-free)

1/2 cup almonds
1/2 to 3/4 cup water
1/4 tsp garlic powder
1 cup olive oil
3 tbsp lemon juice
1/2 tsp apple cider vinegar
3/4 tsp sea salt

1. Cover almonds with boiling water, allow to cool slightly.
2. Slip off skins and have all other ingredients ready.
3. Place almonds in blender or food processor and grind to a fine powder. Add half the water along with garlic powder and salt.
4. Blend well, then add remaining water until mixture is creamy.
5. With blender running low, remove lid insert and drizzle in the oil in a thin stream until mixture is thick.
6. Keep blender running and add lemon juice and vinegar.
7. Blend on low 1 minute longer to allow mixture to thicken to desired consistency.
8. Scrape into a screw-top jar and refrigerate.

This will keep 10 days to 2 weeks.

Note: If you have trouble digesting oil, eliminate the oil completely and increase the water. Will yield 2 cups.

Mushroom/Onion Gravy

2 tbsp olive oil
1 small onion
2 1/2 cups water
1 tsp tamari sauce
1 tsp organic white or yellow miso paste
2 tbsp cornstarch
1/2 tsp dried thyme
1/2 tsp dried rosemary
1/4 tsp dried sage
1 bay leaf
4 oz shitake mushrooms, sliced

1. Sauté onions in saucepan with 2 tbsp olive oil for 5 minutes.
2. Mix cornstarch with small amount of cold water (3 to 4 tbsp) to make a smooth white liquid.
3. Slowly add to onion mixture, continuously stirring.
4. Add remaining ingredients.
5. Cover partially with lid and continue to stir occasionally until sauce thickens (20 minutes).

DELICIOUS, NUTRITIOUS AND SIMPLE

Delicious Gravy for Cooked Vegetables or Grains

1 1/2 cups water
1/2 cup nutritional yeast
1/4 cup tahini
1/8 onion
1 garlic clove, crushed
3 tbsp tamari sauce
1/2 tsp garlic powder
1/2 tsp dried basil
1/2 tsp dried oregano

1. Combine water, nutritional yeast and tahini in blender at medium speed for 1 minute.
2. Add remaining ingredients and blend well at high speed.
3. Add more water to thin or tahini to thicken.
4. Pour gravy into saucepan, warm and stir constantly until heated.

Dips & Spreads

Dips and spreads can be the protein component of lunch when served with raw veggie sticks (especially easy to munch if on the run).

For a filling snack, try dips and spreads on flaxseed, corn, or almond crackers. Remember, snacks can be high-nutrient as well as delicious.

Cashew Nut Paté

1 1/2 cups whole cashews, soaked for 2 hours,
   drained and rinsed
2 tbsp fresh lemon juice
1 small green onion, minced
1 tbsp fresh basil, tarragon, parsley or dill, minced
1/2 tsp sea salt
1/4 to 1/2 cup water to thin to desired consistency
1 garlic clove, crushed

1. Place all ingredients in food processor or blender and mix until smooth (spread should have the consistency of ricotta cheese).
2. Taste for seasonings. Adjust salt and lemon if needed.

Can be used in place of mayonnaise, or thinned and used as a sauce.

Lemon/Garlic Hummus

2 cups chickpeas, cooked or sprouted
4 garlic cloves
1/3 cup tahini (sesame butter)
1/2 cup freshly squeezed lemon juice (2 to 3 lemons)
2 tbsp olive oil
few dashes of paprika
1 1/2 tsp sea salt
freshly ground pepper to taste

1. Place beans and garlic in a food processor and purée, adding the tahini, lemon juice, sea salt, ground pepper and paprika.

DELICIOUS, NUTRITIOUS AND SIMPLE

2. With the machine running, slowly drizzle the olive oil through the tube until the hummus is smooth.

Hummus is a great protein dip for your favorite vegetables, dehydrated flax crackers, rice crackers, or alongside your meal.

Lentil Paté Dip

1/2 cup red lentils
1 1/2 cups water
1/2 medium onion, chopped
1 medium carrot, grated
1 garlic clove, crushed
1 tsp ground cumin
1/2 tsp turmeric
2 tbsp tamari sauce
2 tbsp olive oil
1/2 cup cilantro, finely chopped

1. Place lentils and water in saucepan and bring to boil. Then cover and simmer for 40 minutes.
2. In a cast-iron frying pan, heat oil until just before smoking, then reduce heat.
3. Add onion, carrot and garlic, and sauté, stirring until carrots are soft.
3. Remove from heat and add in remaining ingredients.
4. Stir in cooked red lentils and allow paté to cool before serving.

Simple Salsa

2 cups roma or cherry tomatoes, finely chopped
1/2 red onion, chopped
6 sprigs of cilantro, chopped
12 kalamata olives, pitted and chopped
salt and pepper to taste

Mix all ingredients together and serve.

Pistachio Spread

1 cup pistachio nuts
small chunk of red onion
1/4 cup fresh basil

1 tbsp tamari sauce
1/2 cup water

1. In blender, finely chop nuts.
2. Add remaining ingredients and process again, adding water as needed until until well-blended.

Guacamole

1 ripe avocado, scooped out of skin and pitted
1 tbsp onion, chopped
juice of 1/2 lime or lemon
1 garlic clove, crushed
1 tbsp tamari sauce

1. Mix all ingredients in blender until smooth.
2. Add water if a thinner consistency is desired.

DELICIOUS, NUTRITIOUS AND SIMPLE

Pea Guacamole

3 cups fresh or frozen peas, completely defrosted
1 garlic clove, crushed
2 spring onions, chopped
1 tsp lime juice
1/2 tsp ground cumin
1 tbsp olive oil
2 tbsp fresh cilantro, chopped
black pepper
pinch of cayenne
1 tsp tamari sauce

1. Mix all ingredients in food processor or blender until smooth.
2. Add a little water if too thick.

Tofu Egg(less) Salad Dip & Spread

1 lb firm organic tofu
2 tbsp prepared mustard
1 tbsp tamari sauce
1/2 tsp turmeric
4 scallions, finely chopped
1 celery stalk, finely chopped

1. Drain tofu and mash in a bowl.
2. Add all other ingredients, mixing well.
3. Chill at least 1 hour before serving.

Main Courses

Dinner is the reward at the end of the day, a time to replenish the nutrients used during the afternoon. It is also the time to gather the rich supply of resources needed for deep repair and regeneration work that intensify once we fall asleep and surrender our body to its inner intelligence. If the food eaten contains minimal nutrients, then the body only does its basic renewal work for the next day. If the food is abundant and rich with nutrients, not only does the body do its renewing magic, but it has the opportunity to restore to health any area in the body that is sluggish or in need of repair.

Starting dinner with a salad always guarantees plentiful and varied nutrients, since raw, unprocessed foods contain the highest amounts. Once you start cooking food, its nutrients decrease. Simple cooking will still retain good nutrients, but deep-frying and frozen or canned foods greatly lessen the amount. The only exception is canned or frozen cooked beans.

Most of these recipes make 4 servings.

Vegetable Lasagna

2 cups tomato purée (finely chopped tomatoes)
1/2 tsp oregano
2 garlic cloves, crushed
4 large potatoes, sliced 1/4 inch thick
1 large eggplant, sliced 1/4 inch thick
1 large onion, sliced
2 cups chard, chopped
2 zucchini, sliced 1/4 inch thick
olive oil as needed
1/2 cup water

Optional: 1 cup almond mozzarella cheese, grated

Preheat oven to 400°F.

1. Grease bottom and sides of an 8-inch casserole dish with olive oil.
2. In a bowl, mix together the tomato purée, oregano and garlic. Spread 2 tbsp of tomato purée mixture on bottom of casserole dish.
3. Place one layer of potato slices on top, followed by a layer of eggplant slices, and top with a thin layer of tomato purée.
4. Repeat the same layers two more times, reserving some purée for the top.
5. Follow with a layer of onion slices, then a layer of chard.
6. Finish with a top layer of zucchini.
7. Add remaining tomato purée on top. Sprinkle with 1/4 cup water.
8. Cover with foil and bake for 50 minutes. Remove foil and add almond mozzarella on top. Continue baking another 10 minutes.

DELICIOUS, NUTRITIOUS AND SIMPLE

Brown Rice or Quinoa & Vegetables Garnished with Avocado

2 cups brown rice or quinoa

2 zucchini, chopped

1 large carrot, chopped

4 chard leaves, chopped

1 onion, chopped

1 cup corn kernels (frozen or fresh)

1 cup string beans, chopped

6 cups water

1 avocado, chopped

1. Bring water to boil, add brown rice or quinoa. Cover and simmer for 35 minutes (for brown rice), or about 15 minutes (for quinoa).
2. Add veggies on top and continue cooking another 10 minutes until all water is absorbed.
3. Garnish with chopped avocado.

Quinoa Caviar

1 eggplant

1 onion, minced

1 tbsp olive oil

1 cup quinoa

2 cups water

pinch of salt

1/2 cup fresh herbs, minced (mint, cilantro,
   or whatever you have on hand)

1 tbsp organic white or yellow miso paste
   or 2 tsp tamari sauce

2 tsp lemon juice

Preheat oven to 425°F.

1. Cut eggplant in half, drizzle with olive oil, and bake at 425°F until white flesh is lightly browned and tender (about 30 minutes).
2. Sauté onions in olive oil until soft. Add quinoa and stir for 1 minute.
3. Add water and salt, then bring to a boil. Cover the pan, reduce heat and simmer for 15 minutes. Remove pot from heat and let stand for 10 minutes; remove lid, let cool, and fluff with fork.
4. Purée the eggplant with herbs, miso, and lemon and add to quinoa. Garnish with remaining herbs.

Courtesy of Terri Hall

Spaghetti Squash with Tomato/Veggie Sauce

1 large spaghetti squash

Preheat oven to 350°F.

DELICIOUS, NUTRITIOUS AND SIMPLE

1. Make several fork holes in squash and bake for 1 hour.
2. When squash is cooked, cut through the middle, not lengthwise. Scoop out and discard seeds.
3. With fork, pull out spaghetti-like strands and place on platter.
4. Pour tomato veggie sauce on top and toss.

Optional: Sprinkle with crumbled goat feta or grated almond mozzarella cheese before serving.

Tomato/Veggie Sauce

2 cups tomatoes, fresh and chopped, or 1 16 oz can organic tomatoes, chopped

1 medium-size eggplant, chopped into 1/2 inch cubes

1 zucchini, chopped

4 to 6 shiitake mushrooms, coarsely chopped

1 onion, chopped

1 carrot, finely chopped

2 garlic cloves, crushed

1 tsp oregano

water

2 tbsp tamari sauce

1 tbsp olive oil

Optional: 1 cup soft tofu, crumbled into sauce

1. Place ingredients (except olive oil and tamari sauce) in a pot with 1 1/2 inches of water. Bring to boil, then cover and simmer 35 minutes.
2. Before serving, mix in olive oil and tamari sauce.

This recipe also can be blended when finished, creating a smooth tomato sauce. (Blended tomato sauce is great for kids who don't like the sight of vegetables!)

Quick Chili

1/2 cup water
2 onions, chopped
1 green pepper, chopped
1 celery stalk, chopped
1 garlic clove, crushed
4 cups tomatoes, fresh or canned
4 cups kidney beans, cooked
2 tbsp chili powder
2 tbsp ground cumin
olive oil as needed

1. In a frying pan sauté onions, green pepper, celery and garlic in a small amount of olive oil for 5 minutes.
2. Add remaining ingredients, cover and simmer for another 25 minutes. Stir occasionally. Can be served over brown rice or baked potato.

Zucchini Tabbouleh (non-grain)

5 medium zucchini, peeled
1 large bunch fresh flat-leaf parsley, leaves only
1 large bunch fresh mint, leaves only
3 large tomatoes, peeled, seeded, and chopped
7 scallions, white and green parts, thinly sliced
1/4 cup freshly squeezed lemon juice (about 1 lemon)
1 medium shallot, minced
1 clove garlic
1/4 cup olive oil
sea salt and freshly ground pepper to taste

DELICIOUS, NUTRITIOUS AND SIMPLE

1. In a food processor, pulse the zucchini to the consistency of couscous, then transfer to a large bowl.
2. Chop the parsley and mint leaves in the food processor and add to the zucchini.
3. Stir in the tomatoes and scallions.
4. In a small bowl, mix the lemon juice, shallot, garlic, and oil. Pour over the vegetables and mix well.
5. Chill for at least 30 minutes, or up to 4 hours.
6. Season with salt and pepper before serving.

Courtesy of Kendal Conrad

Pizza à la Healthy

You can choose a crust from one of the two pizza crust recipes. They are both delicious!

Pizza Topping Sauce

1/2 tsp dried oregano
1 cup tomato purée (3 or 4 blended tomatoes)
1/2 small onion, chopped
Optional
1 cup shitake mushrooms, sliced
1 garlic clove, crushed
1/4 cup kalamata olives, sliced
1/2 red bell pepper, sliced into thin strips
1 cup pre-steamed eggplant chunks or zucchini slices
1 cup grated almond or tofu mozzarella cheese

1. Place all ingredients (except the veggie cheese) in a saucepan, bring to boil, then cover and simmer for 5 minutes.

2. Spread pizza sauce on top of crust and sprinkle with almond or tofu mozzarella cheese.
3. Bake according to crust directions.

Polenta Pizza Crust

2/3 cup polenta flour
water
1 tbsp olive oil

Preheat oven to 400°F.

1. Mix polenta flour with 2/3 cup cold water in a pan.
2. Add 2 1/2 cups of boiling water, mixing continuously.
3. Bring to a boil and simmer over low heat, continuing to stir for 5 minutes.
4. Beat in the olive oil.
5. Grease a 10- to 12-inch pizza pan and spread polenta mixture to form pizza crust.
6. Spread sauce on top.
7. Bake in oven for 30 minutes.
8. Sprinkle with grated almond or tofu mozzarella cheese, and let cook for 3 more minutes.

Crispy Almond Pizza Crust

1 large egg
1 tsp olive oil
1 cup almond flour
1/4 tsp kosher salt

1. In a bowl with a wooden spoon, mix all the ingredients well and form a ball.

DELICIOUS, NUTRITIOUS AND SIMPLE

2. Using a parchment-covered baking sheet or an oiled pizza pan, press the dough into a round pizza shape with your hands.
3. Spread on Pizza Topping Sauce (page 53).
4. Put the pizza in a cold oven and heat to 300°F. Cook until pizza crust starts to get golden brown.
5. Sprinkle grated almond or tofu mozzarella cheese on top and cook another 3 minutes.

From Kendall Conrad's book, Eat Well, Feel Well

Baked Falafels

2 cups garbanzo beans, cooked

1 potato, baked or steamed

3 tbsp tahini or sesame butter

1/2 cup parsley

1/2 onion, minced

2 garlic cloves, finely chopped and crushed

1 tbsp tamari sauce

1 tsp paprika

Preheat oven to 350°F.

1. Mash cooked potato, and then purée garbanzo beans in blender.
2. Add all ingredients in a bowl and mix together.
3. Drop spoonfuls of falafel batter on a baking pan greased with olive oil, and bake for 25 minutes.

Can be served on top of a salad, on almond bread, or stuffed inside a red (or savoy) cabbage leaf with chopped tomato and tahini sauce.

Roasted Root Vegetables

Serves 4 to 6

> 2 large carrots (mixed colors), tops removed
> and peeled or scrubbed
> 1 large yam
> 1 lb potatoes
> 1 lb other assorted root vegetables (turnips, parsnips,
> beets, and so on), cleaned
> 1 onion, peeled and quartered
> 1/8 cup olive oil
> 1 tbsp rosemary, oregano and thyme, finely chopped
> 1 tsp sea salt and pepper to taste

Preheat oven to 400°F.

1. Cut carrots, potatoes, yam, and root vegetables into 1-inch pieces.
2. Toss with onion in large bowl with olive oil, herbs, salt and pepper, making sure all are coated evenly.
3. Add vegetables into large shallow roasting pan, spreading them out in a single layer.
4. Roast for 30 minutes, then stir mixture. Continue roasting for another 20 to 30 minutes or until all the vegetables are soft and slightly browned.

DELICIOUS, NUTRITIOUS AND SIMPLE

Tofu Cutlets

2 8-oz cakes tofu

2 tbsp tamari sauce

1 cup nutritional yeast

1/2 tsp olive oil

1/4 tsp basil

1/4 tsp oregano

1 large onion, chopped fine

2 cloves garlic, crushed

Preheat oven to 325°F.

1. Drain tofu well and cut into 1/4-inch-thick slices.
2. Sauté onions and garlic in olive oil until golden.
3. Mix onion mixture together with tamari, oil, and spices.
4. Place tofu slices in mixture and let marinate for 30 minutes.
5. Dip slices in nutritional yeast to coat.
6. Place tofu pieces on oiled cookie sheet and bake for 6 minutes on each side, then broil until crispy. This dish can also be cooked in a frying pan with a little oil.

Fish Main Courses

Fish are an excellent source of protein. Wild-caught (not farmed) fish also contain high amounts of the healing fats known as omega-3 oils.

Choosing the right fish to eat is also a matter of avoiding mercury exposure and supporting our environment. Among wild-caught fish, some of the more healthful choices include Alaskan salmon, mahi mahi, halibut, herring, mackerel, sardines, and cod.

Recipes are for 4 servings.

Pecan-Encrusted Fish

1 1/2 lbs wild-caught white fish
  (mahi-mahi, halibut, or other white fish)
1 cup pecans
1/2 cup lemon juice
2 tbsp tamari sauce
2 garlic cloves, crushed
olive oil as needed

Preheat oven to 350°F.

1. In blender, blend pecans into small pieces. Place on a flat plate.
2. Mix together lemon juice, tamari sauce, and crushed garlic and pour over both sides of fish.
3. Press fish into pecan mixture, coating both sides.
4. Press remaining pecan pieces on top of fish. Place into glass baking dish greased with olive oil, and bake for 15 to 20 minutes.

Baked Wild Salmon with Lemon & Dill

1 1/2 lbs wild-caught salmon
1 lemon
2 garlic cloves, crushed
small bunch fresh dill, chopped
black pepper to taste
olive oil as needed

If salmon is frozen, defrost in package in cold water for 1 hour.

Preheat oven to 350°F.

1. Place fish in a baking pan greased with olive oil.
2. Squeeze lemon over fish and coat with crushed garlic.
3. Sprinkle with black pepper and dill, and add a little olive oil.
4. Cover and bake for 15 minutes. Check to see if cooked in middle.

Poached Wild Salmon

1. Marinate salmon with same ingredients as Baked Wild Salmon with Lemon & Dill (page 60).
2. Coat a cast-iron frying pan thinly with olive oil and add 1 inch water.
3. Bring to a boil and place marinated fish in pan. Cover and simmer about 8 minutes. Test to see if finished (cooking time depends on thickness of fillet).

Coconut/Macadamia Crusted Halibut

1 lb Alaskan wild-caught halibut or other firm, wild, white fish
3/4 cup macadamia nuts, finely chopped
3/4 cup coconut, finely shredded
coconut oil
1 egg white, beaten

1. Mix macadamia nuts and coconut together.
2. Dip fish in egg white and dredge in nut and coconut mixture.
3. Heat coconut oil in an iron skillet.
4. Place fish in heated oil and sauté on both sides until cooked (depending on the thickness of the fish, from 6 to 12 minutes). Be sure not to overcook.

Courtesy of Catherine Gautier-Downs

Halibut with Sun-Dried Tomato & Olive Tapenade

2 lbs wild-caught halibut, washed and patted dry

1 package organic sun-dried tomatoes, sulfur-free
(follow instructions on package as you may need
to soak for 10 minutes in hot water)

1 cup kalamata olives

1/3 cup olive oil

freshly ground black pepper

2 cloves garlic

1/4 cup fresh basil (when in season)

Preheat oven to 375°F.

1. Season halibut with black pepper and place in a glass baking dish. Drizzle with a little olive oil.
2. Place the olives, already soaked sun-dried tomatoes, olive oil, garlic and basil in a food processor or blender. Blend until smooth or pulse until a chunky consistency, depending on your preference.
3. Coat fish top and bottom with half of the tapenade, cover and bake for 15 minutes.
4. Uncover and add more tapenade and bake for 5 minutes until done.

Courtesy of Vanesza Girard

DELICIOUS, NUTRITIOUS AND SIMPLE

Broiled Orange/Mustard-Glazed Salmon

4 wild-caught salmon fillets, skin removed
1 lemon
1 tbsp grated orange zest
1/2 cup freshly squeezed orange juice (about 1 orange)
4 tbsp olive oil
2 tbsp grain mustard
3 cloves garlic, minced
salt and freshly ground pepper to taste

1. Place zest, juice, 2 tbsp oil, mustard, garlic, salt and pepper in a blender or food processor and process until smooth. Set aside. (Can be made one day in advance.)
2. Preheat broiler.
3. Season fish with squeezed lemon juice, followed by sea salt and pepper.
4. Drizzle some of the orange glaze over salmon and reserve the rest of the sauce for later. Let fish marinate for 30 minutes to 1 hour or more if you have time.
5. Broil for 2 to 4 minutes on each side, depending on the thickness of the fish.
6. Brush the salmon with more of the orange glaze and broil for another 3 minutes until golden and cooked to medium.

Courtesy of Vanesza Girard

Cioppino: Italian Fish Stew

1 1/2 lbs wild-caught white fish
(mahi-mahi, halibut, sea bass or other wild-caught fish)
4 roma tomatoes, chopped, or 8 oz can organic
chopped tomatoes
20 kalamata olives, pitted and chopped
1/4 cup fresh dill, chopped
1 small onion, chopped
1 zucchini, chopped
20 string beans, chopped
3 chard leaves, chopped
black pepper to taste
2 cups water
2 tbsp olive oil
tamari sauce

1. Place fish, all vegetables, black pepper and water in large pot,
   bring to boil, then cover and simmer for 20 minutes.
2. Add olive oil and tamari sauce to taste.

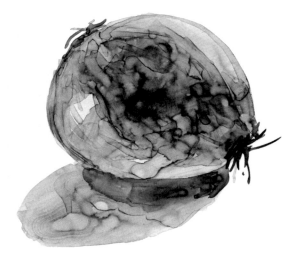

DELICIOUS, NUTRITIOUS AND SIMPLE

Mahi Mahi Fillets with Miso Sauce

1 1/2 lbs wild-caught mahi mahi fillets

2 tsp organic white or yellow miso paste

1 lemon, juiced

2 tsp toasted sesame oil

1 large shallot, diagonally sliced

1 garlic clove, crushed

2 scallions, sliced

8 snow peas

2 tbsp fresh dill, chopped

1. Mix miso and lemon juice.
2. Place oil in pan and heat. Sauté shallot, garlic, and one scallion for 2 to 3 minutes over medium heat.
3. Add fillets, snow peas, dill, and other scallion.
4. Pour miso mixture over fillets. Cover and cook gently for 10 minutes.

Tasty Vegetables

Vegetables! What gifts of the earth! They are rich in vitamins and minerals, plus energy-producing wholesome carbs, along with protein and even small amounts of healthy fats. Most vegetables are about 70 percent water, adding hydration and cleansing to our bodies. Each color is yet another facet: a bounty of specific nutrients, such as iron in beets, folic acid from foliage (as in leafy greens), and carotenes in orange butternut squashes. Choosing a palette of different colored vegetables increases nutrient variety in any meal.

As strong vegetable fiber yields to cooking, the easiest and most nutrient-preservative way is simple steaming. Other cooking methods also have benefits, as well as offer a diversity of tastes and textures. An abundance of vegetables is core for any healthful way of eating, from the Paleo diet to macrobiotics. Partake and enjoy!

Recipes are for 2 servings.

Fresh Steamed Veggies

Select a variety of vegetables, such as:

Group 1: Leafy greens: chard, spinach, collard greens, beet greens, kale
Steam for about 5 minutes until greens become limp.

Group 2: Broccoli, cauliflower, brussel sprouts, string beans, bok choy, cabbage, peas, corn, eggplant, onions, zucchini, leeks, bell peppers
Steam for about 8 minutes until softened.

Group 3: Beets, parsnips, carrots, turnips, hard squashes
Steam for about 12 minutes until softened.

1. Choose from 1/2 to 1 lb mixed vegetables per person, combining a rich array of different colors and textures.
2. If you've chosen vegetables from Group 3, begin steaming them first.
3. After 4 minutes, add vegetables from Group 2.
4. After another 3 minutes, add vegetables from Group 1. Continue cooking for another 5 minutes until done.
5. Cut larger vegetables into smaller bite-sized pieces.
6. Sprinkle with olive oil and lemon juice, or Lemon/Herb Dressing (page 35).

To balance the meal nutritionally, serve vegetables with a food high in complex carbohydrates (potatoes, yams, whole grains or beans) or concentrated protein (fish, beans, tofu or tempeh).

Roasted Mixed Vegetables

The process of roasting brings out the natural sweetness in vegetables and intensifies their natural flavors.

1 large onion, sliced thickly
12 brussel sprouts, cut in half
1 medium eggplant, cut in 1/2 inch slices
6 garlic cloves, peeled
2 red, orange or yellow peppers, cut in thick 1/2 inch strips
bunch of asparagus
1 large zucchini, cut in 3/4 inch slices
salt and pepper
Herbes de Provence

Preheat oven to 400°F.

1. In a large mixing bowl, place all veggies and garlic.
2. Add the oil, toss and coat.
3. Place in oiled glass casserole dish or cookie tray.
4. Roast for 15 minutes and stir vegetables.
5. Continue roasting for another 15 to 25 minutes. Watch closely and remove veggies that are cooked and have softened and browned slightly.
6. When finished, sprinkle with salt and pepper and Herbes de Provence.

Eggplant Chips

1 large eggplant   olive oil   sea salt

1. Slice eggplant into thin rounds, brush with oil and sprinkle with salt.
2. Bake at 400°F for about 20 minutes until crisp, turning when brown.

Steamed Artichokes

2 artichokes

1. Wash artichokes and remove stems.
2. Place heads down in large steaming pot. Steam until bottom of artichoke is tender when poking a fork (usually about 20 minutes).
3. Serve with Artichoke Dipping Sauce (page 36).

Sautéed/Steamed Vegetables, Oriental Style

1 small eggplant, cut into 1/2-inch pieces
1/2 onion, sliced and separated
1 carrot, sliced
1/2 cup broccoli, cut into little tree-like florets
1/2 cup cauliflower, cut into little tree-like florets
big handful of green beans, cut into 1-inch pieces
1 zucchini, sliced
1 cup bean sprouts
2 tbsp olive oil
water
1 tbsp tamari sauce
1/2 tbsp toasted sesame oil

1. Heat olive oil in cast-iron fry pan.
2. Add eggplant, onion and carrot, stirring for 2 minutes.
3. Mix in the remaining vegetables.
4. Add 1/2 inch of water, cover with lid, and simmer 6 minutes.
5. Sprinkle with tamari sauce and toasted sesame oil.

DELICIOUS, NUTRITIOUS AND SIMPLE

Vegetable Purée

This is delicious on baked potatoes or as a side dish by itself.

1 cup broccoli
1 cup cauliflower
1/2 small onion
1/2 cup water
1/2 lemon, juiced
1 tbsp tamari sauce

Other vegetables can be added such as corn, carrots, zucchini, butternut squash, or beets.

1. Steam vegetables lightly (about 8 minutes).
2. Put in blender and purée until smooth.

Festive String Beans with Toasted Almonds

1 lb string beans with ends cut off
24 raw almonds, sliced or coarsely chopped
olive oil
1 tbsp tamari sauce
black pepper, freshly ground

1. Heat a cast iron fry pan to medium, add almonds and continuously stir until they turn a golden color. Remove and place in a cup.
2. Heat pan again and coat bottom thinly with oil.
3. Add string beans and coat with oil.

4. Stir in tamari sauce and add 1/4 inch of water. Cover and simmer until beans are tender, but not soft. Remove from heat, add pepper and roll in toasted almonds.

Ratatouille

2 tomatoes, chopped

1 zucchini, chopped

1 eggplant, cut in 1/2-inch chunks

1/2 onion, chopped

2 leaves chard, chopped

10 kalamata olives, pitted and sliced

1 clove garlic, crushed

dash of oregano

2 tbsp olive oil

water as needed

1. Place all ingredients, except olive oil, in pot with 1 inch of water and stir.
2. Bring to a boil, then cover and simmer 10 minutes.
3. When finished, mix in olive oil.

Spaghetti Squash Tossed in Olive Oil & Garlic

1 medium-sized spaghetti squash

4 tbsp olive oil

3 garlic cloves, crushed

1/8 tsp black pepper

2 tbsp tamari sauce

DELICIOUS, NUTRITIOUS AND SIMPLE

Preheat oven to 375°F.

1. Wash spaghetti squash and pierce 5 times with a fork. Bake in oven for 1 hour.
2. When squash is cooked, cut through the middle, not lengthwise. Scoop out and discard seeds.
3. With a fork, pull out spaghetti-like strands and place on platter.
4. Heat oil, add garlic and cook about 2 minutes until garlic begins to crisp slightly.
5. Remove from heat and add tamari sauce and pepper, and toss with squash until thoroughly coated.

Basil Pesto for Spaghetti Squash

This is a versatile pesto sauce that can also be used with fish, potatoes, grilled vegetables, or spaghetti squash. It's up to you!

1 cup pine nuts
4 to 6 garlic cloves
2 cups organic basil leaves, washed and rinsed
squeeze of lemon
1/2 cup olive oil
sea salt and freshly ground pepper to taste

1. Place pine nuts and garlic in food processor and blend.
2. Add a squeeze of lemon and basil leaves.
3. Slowly drizzle olive oil through the feed tube and blend again until smooth.
4. Season with sea salt and pepper to taste.

Courtesy of Vanesza Girard

Potato & Yam Dishes

In the past decade, with more and more new dietary fads in the marketplace, potatoes have gotten a bad rap. They have been placed in the category of refined carbohydrates, and they absolutely are not. Potatoes and yams are both 70 percent water, highly alkaline, and filled with good fiber, vitamins and minerals, especially vitamin C in potatoes and vitamin A in yams. They make excellent cleansing meals — meals with a high volume of water to give the body an extra flush. It is beneficial to have one of these foods once or twice a week to support cleansing and balance.

Recipes are for 4 servings.

Baked French Fries

1 lb potatoes per person, sliced 1/4-inch thick
natural mustard to taste, or ketchup, sugar-free

Preheat oven to 475°F.
1. Place potato slices on oven rack for 20 minutes
   or until slightly brown and puffy.
2. Season with mustard or ketchup.

Mashed Potatoes

4 potatoes, medium-size, peeled
and cut into large chunks
1 small onion, chopped
1 garlic clove, crushed
water as needed
1 tbsp olive oil
Optional: 4 tbsp parsley, chopped

1. Place all ingredients in saucepan (except olive oil) and add
   1 1/2 inches of water.
2. Bring to a boil, then cover and simmer for another 20 minutes,
   checking after 12 minutes to make sure the water has not
   evaporated.
3. Remove from heat and pour with liquid into blender.
   Add olive oil and blend until smooth.
4. Serve with Mushroom/Onion Gravy (page 38).

Parsley Potatoes

4 large potatoes, cut in quarters
1 cup parsley, chopped
black pepper to taste
sprinkle of olive oil

1. Steam potatoes until soft.
2. Cut into smaller chunks.
3. Sprinkle with parsley, black pepper, and olive oil. Toss and serve.

Baked Stuffed Potatoes

4 large russet or Yukon gold potatoes
1 small onion, chopped
8 kalamata olives, pitted and chopped
1 tbsp olive oil
1 avocado

Preheat oven to 350°F.

1. Wash potatoes and bake for 1 hour in oven.
2. Sauté onion and olives together for 5 minutes in olive oil.
3. Split potatoes in half. Scoop out contents and place in bowl with onion/olive mixture.
4. Mash with avocado.
6. Fill potatoes with warm mixture and serve immediately.

Baked Yams with Orange

1 lb yams per person
1 sweet orange, cut in half

Preheat oven to 350°F.

1. Prick yams with a fork and bake 1 hour in the oven. (Place a sheet of aluminum foil in bottom of oven to catch drippings.)
2. Slice yams open and squeeze orange juice into yams and mash with fork.

Yam/Orange Cups

4 yams, medium-size
4 oranges
2 oz pecans, chopped
8 whole pecans

Preheat oven to 350°F.

1. Bake yams 1 hour until tender.
2. Cut oranges in half and scoop out insides.
3. Place orange pulp in blender and blend slightly.
4. When yams are cooked, scoop out insides and place in mixing bowl.
5. Add pecans and 1 cup orange pulp and mash together.
6. Fill orange halves with mixture, forming a round cone on top.
7. With fork create circular texture, and top each yam-stuffed orange with one whole pecan.
8. Place orange cups on baking tray and place under broiler a few minutes to reheat.

DELICIOUS, NUTRITIOUS AND SIMPLE

Potato Latkes

Makes 20 to 24 small-to-medium cakes

2 lbs potatoes, grated
1 medium onion, finely chopped
1/2 cup chickpea flour
1/2 tsp dulse flakes
salt and pepper to taste

1. Mix grated potatoes, onion, and salt in a bowl and let stand 5 minutes. Empty excess water.
2. Stir potato mixture with the rest of the ingredients.
3. Heat a cast-iron skillet on low/medium heat, greased with olive oil .
4. Hand pat thin patties (the thinner they are, the faster they will cook).
5. Flip once until both sides are brown and crispy.

Potato Stew

3 large potatoes, cut into 1/2-inch chunks
1 medium onion, chopped   1 zucchini, chopped
handful of string beans, chopped   2 tomatoes, chopped
salt and pepper to taste   2 tbsp olive oil
1/4 tsp oregano   handful of fresh parsley or dill, chopped

1. Place all ingredients (except olive oil) in a large pot and add 2 inches of water.
2. Bring to a boil, cover and simmer for 15 minutes.
3. Add salt, pepper, and olive oil to taste.

Option: Can be blended for creamy potato porridge.

Soups

Ah, soups...one-pot meals, soothing, with always some left over for the next day. No wonder we all love soup! Sometimes I even have soup for breakfast and usually garnish it with some avocado to add the balance of good fats and keep me full until lunch.

Organic white or yellow miso paste is a great bouillon for seasoning and saltiness. Made of fermented soy, it is easy to digest and has probiotic healthful bacteria to assist with digestion. For this reason, it is always better to add the miso after the soup has been cooked, so that the higher heat doesn't wipe out the extra health benefits.

In these recipes you will find both simple soups and more complex soups. The simple soups have all the ingredients cooked in water from the start. In the more complex recipes, some of the vegetables are sautéed before being added to the soup.

Recipes are for 4 servings.

Simple Butternut Squash Soup

 1 medium butternut squash, peeled, seeded
  and cut into 1-inch chunks
 1 small onion, coarsely chopped
 1 medium carrot, coarsely chopped
 1 medium zucchini, coarsely chopped
 1 cup corn kernels, cooked
 6 sprigs fresh dill, chopped, or 1/2 tsp dried dill weed
 sea salt, pepper, and tamari sauce

1. Place all ingredients (except salt, pepper, and tamari sauce)
   in pot. Add just enough water to barely cover.
2. Cover with lid and bring to a boil, then simmer 10 minutes.
2. Liquefy with hand-held mixer or in a blender. Add salt,
   tamari sauce and pepper to taste.

Fancy Gazpacho

*Refreshing and nutrient-rich gazpacho makes for a deliciously
cool soup on a warm summer day. I take full advantage of the fresh
vegetables at the farmers market. This can be made to suit your
taste buds, either spicy or not.*

 4 ripe tomatoes, cored, seeded, and cut into 2-inch
  chunks (heirlooms are a nice addition when available)
 1 medium sweet onion or red onion, peeled and
  coarsely chopped
 3 large cucumbers, peeled, seeded, and roughly chopped
 1 large red, orange, or yellow bell pepper, roughly chopped
 2 cloves garlic, minced

DELICIOUS, NUTRITIOUS AND SIMPLE

1/2 cup parsley, finely chopped

1/2 cup cilantro, finely chopped

3/4 cup fresh lemon juice

1/2 cup extra-virgin olive oil

sea salt and freshly ground pepper to taste

Liquefy in blender until desired consistency.

Courtesy of Vanesza Girard

Black Bean & Corn Soup

2 cups black beans, soaked overnight in water
   (or 2 cans cooked organic black beans)

2 carrots, chopped

1 onion, chopped

2 zucchini, chopped

bunch of fresh dill, chopped

2 cups corn kernels

8 cups water, if using soaked beans
   (water to cover if using canned beans)

1 tbsp olive oil

tamari sauce or sea salt to taste

1 avocado

1. Rinse beans, put in pot with water, bring to boil, cover and simmer. Check after 1 hour. (For canned beans, heat to boil, cover and simmer for 20 minutes.)
2. When beans are slightly soft, add remaining ingredients and continue simmering until beans are tender.
3. Add olive oil and tamari sauce or sea salt to taste.
4. Garnish with chopped avocado.

Creamy Red Lentil Soup

1 cup red lentils
1 small onion, chopped
2 chard leaves, chopped
1 carrot, chopped
1 zucchini, chopped
1/2 cup corn kernels, cooked
handful of fresh dill, chopped, or 1/2 tsp dried dill
2 tbsp organic white or yellow miso paste
1 lemon, juiced
1 tbsp olive oil
4 cups water
1/4 to 1/2 avocado, chopped
salt and pepper to taste

1. Bring water to boil, and add lentils. Cover and simmer.
2. After 15 minutes, add all other vegetables, including dill. Cover and simmer for 30 minutes (for red lentils), or 45 minutes (for green lentils, which take longer to dissolve than red lentils). Check after 15 minutes to make sure there is enough water.
3. After lentils are soft, remove 1 cup of liquid and add to it 1 heaping tbsp of miso, mixing until completely dissolved.
4. Add mixture back into soup, along with olive oil and lemon juice, and stir.
5. Serve chopped avocado on top as a garnish.

DELICIOUS, NUTRITIOUS AND SIMPLE

Summer Borscht

3 cups water

2 large beets (including greens),
   cut into large bite-size pieces

2 medium carrots, sliced

1 large onion, cut into large
   bite-sized pieces

4 large new potatoes, cut
   into large bite-sized pieces

Seasoning

1/4 cup lemon juice

1/4 tsp sea salt

pepper to taste

1 tsp paprika

1. Bring water to boil in a large soup pot, then turn down to simmer.
2. Add each vegetable to pot, starting with beets. Cover and simmer 15 minutes.
3. When vegetables are tender, blend the entire mixture, including the broth (the cooking water).
4. If proportions are too dry for blending, add another 1/2 cup extra liquid, such as soup broth or water. The consistency should be thick and slightly coarse.
5. Mix seasoning into soup mixture and chill.

When serving, garnish with 1/2 cup tofu sour cream and 2 chopped scallions.

Courtesy of Nadia Natali, from Cooking Off the Grid

20-Minute Miso/Vegetable/ Lima Bean Soup

1 bag lima beans, frozen
2 carrots, chopped
1 onion, chopped
2 zucchini, chopped
bunch of fresh dill, chopped
1 cup corn kernels
2 tbsp organic white or yellow miso paste
water as needed
1 tbsp olive oil

1. Rinse lima beans and put in pot with chopped vegetables, including dill. Cover with water.
2. Bring to boil, cover and simmer for 20 minutes.
3. Remove 1 cup of liquid and to that add 1 heaping tbsp miso, and mix until completely dissolved.
4. Add mixture back into soup, along with olive oil, and stir.

French Onion Soup

4 medium yellow onions, thickly sliced
1 carrot, diced
pinch of dried oregano
pinch of dried thyme
2 tbsp olive oil
2 tbsp organic white or yellow miso paste
ground pepper

DELICIOUS, NUTRITIOUS AND SIMPLE

1. In a cast-iron fry pan heat oil and sauté onions and carrots over low heat, stirring occasionally.
2. Once the onions are transparent, pour contents of pan into a soup pan and add water to slightly above the vegetable line.
3. Add spices, bring to a boil, then cover and simmer for 20 minutes.
4. Remove 1 cup of liquid and to that add 1 heaping tbsp miso, mixing until completely dissolved.
5. Add mixture back into soup and stir.

Pumpkin/Yam Soup

2 tbsp olive oil
1 tsp fresh ginger, minced
1 garlic clove, minced
1/2 medium onion, diced
3 cups pumpkin, coarsely diced
3 cups yams, coarsely diced
3 cups water or vegetable broth
dash of cumin, nutmeg, cayenne pepper
1 tsp tamari sauce
dash of tarragon
Optional: 1/4 bunch tarragon

1. In soup pan, sauté ginger, garlic, and onion in olive oil.
2. Add pumpkin, yams, spices and water.
3. Cover and simmer for 15 minutes.
4. Purée soup in a blender or use electric hand blender.
5. Add tarragon and let sit for 5 minutes before serving.

Courtesy of Beatrix Rohlsen, from The Art of Taste

Cream of Vegetable Soup

(dairy-free)

Serves 2

1 large onion, coarsely chopped

1 leek, coarsely chopped

2 carrots, coarsely chopped

2 zucchini, coarsely chopped

3 chard leaves, coarsely chopped

2 medium potatoes, coarsely chopped

3 tbsp olive oil

1/2 cup fresh dill, chopped, or 1/4 tsp dried dill

2 tbsp organic white or yellow miso paste

1/2 avocado, chopped

1. Put vegetables in saucepan and add water, leaving 1/2 inch of vegetables above water line.
2. Bring to a boil, then cover and simmer 1/2 hour.
3. Add olive oil and miso. Purée in blender or use a hand-held blender.
4. Sprinkle dill in center of each bowl of soup.
5. Garnish with avocado.

DELICIOUS, NUTRITIOUS AND SIMPLE

Tomato Basil Soup

3 tbsp olive oil
1 onion, finely chopped
2 lb ripe plum tomatoes, roughly chopped
1 garlic clove, pressed
6 1/4 cups water
2 tbsp sun-dried tomato paste
2 tbsp fresh basil, shredded
salt and pepper

1. Heat oil in large saucepan, add onion and sauté 5 minutes, stirring frequently until softened but not brown.
2. Stir in the chopped tomatoes, garlic and water. Bring to boil, then lower heat, half cover pot, and simmer gently for 20 minutes, stirring occasionally.
3. Add salt and pepper to taste.
4. Pour into blender, add basil and blend.

Bread & Crackers

Bread is generally a filler food, meaning it fills one up because it swells in water, as with croutons. We feel satiated by eating bread, but we are not being filled with high-nutrient food. Most breads are processed grain — to differing degrees — that has a reduced amount of vitamins and minerals, therefore diluting the nutrient content of meals they are in.

Then there is the wheat and gluten issue. So many people have gluten allergies and half of them don't even know it! Wheat as we know it today is a highly hybrid variety, and has been implicated in a large number of health issues, from digestive disorders to arthritis.

The following high-nutrient recipes are great substitutes for regular bread and crackers. The crackers are baked in a dehydrator at 110° F to preserve the healthful oils and other nutrients. Some new ovens can actually bake at that temperature.

Almond Bread

Almond bread has only six ingredients and takes less than 10 minutes to make. It is a high-protein, high-fiber bread.

1 lb almonds
2 eggs, beaten*
1 1/2 tsp baking soda
1/2 tsp sea salt
1 tbsp olive oil
3/4 cup carbonated water

* A vegan alternative egg replacement

2 tbsp flax seeds, freshly ground
6 tbsp water
Stir together until gelatinous.

Preheat oven to 350°F.

1. Blend almonds (a small amount at a time) in food processor or blender to fine texture.
2. In a bowl, add remaining ingredients.
3. Pour into olive-oiled bread pan and bake 1 hour.
4. Take out of baking pan and let cool.

Stores in refrigerator for up to two weeks.

Toppings for Almond Bread

Nut butters, fresh persimmon or other fruit, hummus with the following: tomato, onion, cucumber, avocado, or cashew dip.

DELICIOUS, NUTRITIOUS AND SIMPLE

Almond Crackers

2 cups almonds, soaked overnight
1/2 cup sesame seeds
1 clove garlic
1/4 cup parsley, minced
1 cup carrots, shredded
3 green onions, minced
sea salt to taste

1. In a blender or food processor, grind almonds, sesame and garlic.
2. Pour into bowl and add carrots, parsley and onions to mixture.
3. Salt to taste.
4. Spread batter, about 1/4 inch thick, on parchment paper–lined dehydrator trays.
5. Score with a knife into vertical and horizontal lines about 2 inches apart.
6. Dehydrate at 110°F for 12 hours or until dried and crisp.

Corn Crackers

6 ears fresh corn, or 1 lb frozen corn, defrosted
1 small onion, chopped
2 tbsp flax seeds, ground
1 cup sunflower seeds, soaked and hulled
salt and black pepper to taste

1. Blend ingredients in blender or food processor.
2. Drop 2-inch rounds onto parchment paper–lined dehydrator trays.
3. Dehydrate at 110°F for 12 hours or until dried and crisp.

Pumpkin Seed Crackers

2 cups pumpkin seeds, soaked for 6 hours
1/2 red bell pepper, minced
1 zucchini, grated
1/2 cup hulled sesame seeds, soaked for 6 hours
1/4 cup onion, minced
1 tbsp dried oregano and dried dill
1/2 tsp sea salt

1. Put all ingredients in blender or food processor and grind to medium consistency.
2. Spread batter, about 1/4 inch thick, on parchment paper–lined dehydrator trays.
3. Score with a knife into vertical and horizontal lines about 2 inches apart.
4. Dehydrate at 110°F for 12 hours or until dried and crisp.

Flax Seed Crackers

1 1/2 cups red bell pepper, chopped
1/4 cup onion, chopped
2 cloves garlic, crushed
1 tsp lemon juice
1 1/4 tsp sea salt
1/4 cup minced fresh herbs (basil, parsley, dill or oregano)
2 cups flax seeds, soaked 12 hours in 3 1/2 cups water
   (do not rinse or drain)

1. In blender or food processor, grind red bell pepper, onion, garlic, lemon juice, fresh herbs and salt.

DELICIOUS, NUTRITIOUS AND SIMPLE

2. Transfer vegetable mixture to large bowl, add flax seeds and mix.
3. Spread batter, about 1/4 inch thick, on parchment paper–lined dehydrator trays.
4. Score with a knife into vertical and horizontal lines about 2 inches apart.
5. Dehydrate at 110°F for 12 hours or until dried and crisp.

Crunchy Onion & Chia Seed Crackers

2 medium onions (1 finely chopped, 1 thinly sliced)
1 cup chia seeds (white, black, or a mix)
1 cup sunflower seeds, finely ground
1/2 cup olive oil
3 1/2 tbsp tamari

1. Place all ingredients in a large bowl and mix thoroughly.
2. Spread batter, about 1/4 inch thick, on parchment paper–lined dehydrator trays.
3. Score with a knife into vertical and horizontal lines about 2 inches apart.
4. Dehydrate at 110°F for 12 hours or until dried and crisp.

Note: All dehydrated crackers can be stored in air-tight containers for up to three months. If you don't have access to a dehydrator, these recipes can be made in an oven. Bake on the lowest temperature possible for 1 or 2 hours until dried and crisp. Although the higher heat will destroy the omega-3 oils, it will still be a high-protein delicious snack.

Desserts

Desserts...an occasional treat at the end of a meal or to celebrate a special occasion. There is no reason desserts can't be sweet, delicious, and full of high nutrients at the same time.

Desserts should be served sparingly, because even natural sweeteners (dates, fruit, maple syrup, and agave nectar) can add up to too much glucose in the bloodstream. This in itself is a concern for those with diabetes. It can also result in stored fat, an important factor for people who need to lose weight.

It's helpful to know that a small bite, truly tasted and savored, never gets better — in fact, we usually stop paying attention to its taste after the first bite or two. Next time, be sure to notice!

Recipes are for 4 servings unless otherwise stated.

Lime Mousse

Serves 6

4 avocados
1/2 cup light agave nectar, honey, or maple syrup
1/2 cup lime juice   1/4 tsp Celtic or Himalayan salt
1 cup fresh raspberries

1. Place all ingredients, except raspberries, in food processor and process until very smooth and fluffy. Adjust for sweet and tart flavors, which will vary depending on size of avocados.
2. Served chilled, topped with fresh raspberries.

Courtesy of Diane Best

Mango/Chia Pudding

Serves 4

1 14 oz can of organic coconut milk   5 tbsp chia seeds
1/2 lb frozen mango, defrosted
   or 1 large ripe mango, peeled and cut into chunks
dash of cardamom

1. Blend mango until smooth, then pour equal amounts of the purée into four 8 oz jars or parfait glasses.
2. Blend coconut milk until smooth. Pour into mixing bowl.
3. Add chia seeds and cardamom to coconut milk and stir for 3 to 4 minutes until thickened.
4. Pour chia mixture on top of the mango.
5. Cover and refrigerate at least 3 hours before serving.

This will last 4 days in the fridge.

DELICIOUS, NUTRITIOUS AND SIMPLE

Date/Nut Balls

1/2 cup whole raw cashews
1/2 cup dried figs, cut into small pieces
1 cup dried dates, cut into small pieces
1/2 cup raw almonds
1/2 cup dried coconut, finely grated

1. Grind nuts finely in food processor or blender.
2. Add chopped figs and dates, blend again until well-mixed.
3. Shape into little balls with wet hands and roll them in grated coconut.

Courtesy of Beatrix Rohlsen from The Art of Taste

Banana/Mango Ice Cream

4 ripe bananas, peeled and frozen
2 cups mango, frozen
Optional: fresh or frozen berries, blended to use as topping

1. In any juicer with an auger (Champion, Omega 8000 series, Samson, Solo Star II), put in special filter blocking attachment.
2. Feed the bananas and mango into the machine, alternating one, then the other, until all fruit is passed through. Mixture should come out like rich, creamy ice cream.
3. Serve immediately.

Alternatively, the frozen fruit can be blended in a high-speed blender, but may need to be slightly defrosted and have some water added. It will have a consistency more like soft serve or frozen yogurt.

Try many different kinds of frozen fruit and berries, but always use with frozen banana to get smooth, ice cream–like texture.

Raspberry Cheesecake (raw & dairy-free)

Crust

> 2 cups macadamia nuts
> 1/2 cup dates, pitted
> 1/4 cup coconut, dried

1. To make the crust, grind the macadamia nuts and dates in a food processor.
2. Sprinkle dried coconut onto the bottom of an 8- or 9-inch springform pan.
3. Press crust onto the coconut. This will prevent it from sticking.

Cheese Filling

> 3 cups chopped cashews, soaked for at least 1 hour
> 3/4 cup honey
> 3/4 cup lemon juice
> 3/4 cup coconut oil
> 1 tsp vanilla
> *Optional: 1/2 tsp sea salt*

1. Blend the cashews, lemon, honey, gently warmed coconut oil, vanilla, sea salt (if using), and 1/2 cup water. Blend until smooth and adjust to taste.
2. Pour the mixture onto the crust. Remove air bubbles by tapping the pan lightly.
3. Place in freezer until firm. Remove the whole cake from pan while frozen and place on a serving platter. Defrost in the refrigerator. Top with Raspberry Sauce (page 101).

DELICIOUS, NUTRITIOUS AND SIMPLE

Raspberry Sauce

1 bag raspberries, frozen
1/2 cup dates

1. Mix raspberries and dates in a food processor until well blended. (Do not use a blender for this or the raspberry seeds will become grainy.)
2. Spread raspberry sauce on top of cake and serve.

Courtesy of Emily Lee Angell

Almond Coconut Cake

4 cups almond flour
1/2 cup agave syrup or honey
2 tsp baking soda
1 tsp sea salt
1/4 cup coconut oil, plus extra for greasing pans
1/2 cup canned and unsweetened coconut milk
1/4 cup coconut yogurt (dairy-free), or applesauce
3 large egg whites
2 tsp pure vanilla extract

Preheat oven to 300°F.

1. Line the bottom of two 8-inch round cake pans with parchment paper. Use coconut oil to grease the paper and the sides of the pans.
2. In a food processor or electric mixer, mix the almond flour, agave or honey, baking soda, and sea salt until well blended. Add the coconut oil and coconut milk and mix well, stopping to scrape down the sides.

3. Add yogurt, egg whites, and vanilla. Mix well until very smooth, scraping sides frequently.
4. Pour into the cake pans and smooth the tops. Bake for 40 minutes, or until the cakes are golden and springy, and a toothpick inserted in the center of the cake comes out clean.
5. Remove from the oven and let sit for 10 minutes. Unmold from the pans onto a rack and let cool completely before frosting.

Frosting

2/3 cup agave syrup or honey
1/3 cup canned and unsweetened coconut milk
3 tbsp unsalted raw butter
1 tsp pure vanilla extract
3 cups coconut, unsweetened and grated
parchment paper (unbleached)

Place the agave, coconut milk, butter and vanilla in a food processor or electric mixer, and process until smooth.

To assemble the cake

1. Place one of the layers on a serving dish. Spread half of the frosting on the cake and sprinkle with 1 cup grated coconut.
2. Place the second layer on top. Spread the remaining frosting on the top, allowing it to spill over the sides.
3. Sprinkle the rest of the coconut over the cake.

The cake will keep for 3 days in a plastic cake keeper, or on a cake stand with a dome cover.

Variation: Layer fresh sliced strawberries on top of the coconut between the two layers and on top of the cake.

DELICIOUS, NUTRITIOUS AND SIMPLE

Crunchy Maple/Nut Granola Cookies
(oil-free, grain-free)

This is the same recipe as the Breakfast Crunchy Maple/Nut Granola (page 14). The only difference is that when you smooth it on sheets to cook, you score the batter into squares. After it is cooked, you just break the sheet up into delicious cookies…they are the best!

3 cups almonds
3 cups walnuts
3 cups whole cashews
3 cups sunflower seeds
2 cups pumpkin seeds
1 1/2 cups sesame seeds
1 cup pure maple syrup (Grade B)
1 cup fresh apple juice
2 tsp vanilla extract
1 1/2 tsp salt
2 tbsp cinnamon
1 tsp Pumpkin Pie Spice*

1. In a food processor, lightly grind almonds, cashews and walnuts to desired texture (keeping the nuts chunky). Transfer to a large bowl.
2. Add whole pumpkin and sunflower seeds, salt, and dry spices to bowl.
3. Mix maple syrup, apple juice, and vanilla. Pour over nut mixture and mix well by hand to coat everything.
4. Sprinkle in the sesame seeds, and mix well again.
5. Spread 4 cups per sheet on parchment paper-lined dehydrator trays.
6. With a large knife, score mixture on the sheets, both horizontally and vertically every 2 inches.
7. Dehydrate at 110°F for 12 hours or until dried and crisp.

* Available in most stores

8. When dry and crisp, break up sheets into square cookies and store in airtight containers.

Courtesy of Dianne Bess

Note: If you don't have a dehydrator, you can still make this recipe in an oven. Bake on the lowest temperature possible for 1 or 2 hours until dried and crisp. Although the higher heat will destroy the omega-3 oil, it will still be a high-protein delicious meal.

Almond/Coconut Macaroons

Produces about 25 macaroons

> 3 cups dried, unsweetened coconut flakes
> 1/2 cup pure maple syrup (Grade B)
> 1/2 cup coconut butter, melted
> 1 tbsp vanilla extract
> 1/2 tsp sea salt
> 1 1/2 cups almond flour, finely ground

1. In a large bowl, combine all ingredients and stir well.
2. Using a small scoop (1 1/2 tbsp) or your hands, form dough into small balls and arrange close together on a cookie sheet. Place in the refrigerator for 1/2 hour to set, and also for storage (in an air-tight jar). Garnish with lemon zest.
3. Macaroons can be dehydrated instead, at 105°F for 6 to 9 hours, until crisp on the outside and chewy on the inside. Unlike the refrigerated macaroons that need to be kept at a lower temperature, these can be stored in air-tight jars on a shelf.

Courtesy of Raw Food, Real World

DELICIOUS, NUTRITIOUS AND SIMPLE

Stuffed Baked Apples

6 apples, cored (make cone-shaped hole in
    center of apple but not through to bottom)
1 cup walnuts, chopped
2 tsp cinnamon
1 tsp nutmeg
1/2 tsp ground ginger
1 cup dates, pitted
1 cup water
1/4 cup pure maple syrup (Grade B)

Preheat oven to 350°F.

1. Mix walnuts, cinnamon, nutmeg and ginger in bowl and set aside.
2. Combine dates and water in small saucepan. Simmer mixture for 1/2 hour, or until liquid is reduced by half. Combine all ingredients except syrup.
3. Place apples in an appropriately sized baking dish. Fill with walnut and date mixture.
4. Drizzle maple syrup evenly over each apple. Bake uncovered in oven for 1 hour, or until apples are tender.

Courtesy of Simply Good Recipes

Vegetable Juices & Nut Milks

Fresh vegetable juices are the most powerful way to get huge amounts of vitamins and minerals into the body, *fast!* They are not meal substitutes, as they are metabolized very quickly and do not contain fiber. Yet this very quality is what allows juices to radically increase your nutrient intake in a highly efficient way. They are truly vegetable blood.

Since vegetable juice contains the greatest amounts of nutrients (especially intact enzymes) in the first few minutes after juicing, it is best to drink it right away, as well as before eating food. This allows the nutrients to be most rapidly absorbed. To get maximum benefits beyond a highly nutritious way of eating, add at least one freshly made vegetable juice a day to your daily food choices, if not more!

Because high amounts of concentrated nutrients facilitate the body's self-healing mechanisms, many cancer clinics (as well as gyms and health spas) include vegetable juicing as an important part of their healing support.

As for storing, a good amount of nutrients is still preserved if the juice is kept refrigerated in an airtight glass jar for up to 8 hours.

Benefits of Juicing Specific Foods

Carrots are high in carotenes and are great for the eyes, skin and immune system.

Celery and cucumber are kidney flushers. They add a lot of fluid and alkalinity to the juice and help soften the taste. Use the skin of the cucumber if it is unwaxed. The skin is rich in the mineral silica, which is beneficial for bones, skin and hair.

Chard is high in calcium and magnesium, as well as many other minerals.

Cabbage soothes the stomach and can help heal ulcers.

Cilantro chelates heavy metals and helps flush them from the body, especially mercury.

Parsley is high in chlorophyll and minerals.

Beets are super-high in iron and other minerals due to their deep, deep roots and are excellent for the liver. Beware though, juicing more than 1 small beet can cause loose stools for some people. It also can turn urine and stools pinkish, but there is no problem with that. Beet greens are great to juice, too!

Dandelion Greens are powerful liver and kidney supports and cleansers.

Ginger is an anti-inflammatory, and has anti-nausea and calming properties to aid digestion.

Apples provide vitamins, sweetness, and the pectin helps to form loose stools.

Note: Recent research is suggesting that kale, more than any other vegetable, may absorb a toxic metal from the soil, thallium, and therefore should be used only sparingly, perhaps not more than 1 or 2 times a week at most.

All of these juices can remain refrigerated in an airtight container for 8 hours before they start to lose their quality.

Power Juice

2 medium-sized carrots
1/2 cucumber
3 stalks celery
(Juice should be about 1/3 of each ingredient.)
Plus: mix and match with a small chunk of beet,* 1/2 small zucchini, 4 to 6 dandelion leaves, chard or kale leaves, handful of cilantro or parsley, thin slice of ginger root, and 1/2 inch turmeric root

* Beet juice can cause urine or stools to turn reddish, which is not a problem. On the contrary, beet is excellent for the liver and gall bladder. It is best to start with small amounts, like a chunk or a small beet, since it can have a strong laxative effect on some people.

Savory Cocktail

1 tomato, or a handful of cherry tomatoes
1/2 cucumber
4 stalks celery
1 garlic clove
handful of cilantro or parsley
1 chard leaf
2 kale leaves
1/4 lemon, peeled

Green Essence

1/2 cucumber
1/2 zucchini
3 celery stalks
handful of cilantro or parsley

3 leaves dandelion greens
1 chard leaf
handful of spinach

Liver Delight

3 medium-sized carrots
4 stalks celery
1 small beet
5 leaves dandelion greens

handful of cilantro
small slice ginger root
2 chard leaves

Kidney Soother

1 handful cranberries, fresh or frozen
1 whole cucumber
5 leaves dandelion greens

1 carrot
3 celery stalks
1/4 lemon, peeled

Digestive Ease

1/6 large white cabbage
1/2 cucumber
4 celery stalks
handful of parsley

1 carrot
1 slice ginger root
1 Granny Smith apple

DELICIOUS, NUTRITIOUS AND SIMPLE

Leg Cramp Juice

3 leaves romaine lettuce
1 carrot
1/2 cucumber

3 stalks celery
2 chard leaves

Blood Builder Juice

3 kale leaves
4 stalks celery
1 cucumber
2 carrots

1 burdock root
1 small beet
1 handful of spinach

Child's First Juice

*This is a sweet juice that basically tastes like apple juice.
It is an easy way to slip more nutrients into a child's diet.*

1 apple
1 small carrot
1 celery stalk

Almond Milk

Makes 2 cups

> 1 cup almonds, soaked overnight in water
> 2 cups water
> *Optional: 2 to 3 pitted dates, shake of cinnamon,
> or 1/2 tsp alcohol-free vanilla extract*

1. After 8 hours of soaking, rinse almonds and place in blender with 2 cups water and blend until smooth.
2. Strain or squeeze through a fine mesh strainer or bag.
3. Can put almond meal back in blender. Add some more water and blend again.
4. Discard almond meal after the second blend. Milk may be stored up to 3 days in fridge.

For a thicker, richer almond cream, use less water.

Variation: Can be made with a combination of almonds, cashews, brazil nuts, pistachios, sunflower seeds, or filberts. Dates or bananas can be added before blending to sweeten.

DELICIOUS, NUTRITIOUS AND SIMPLE

Vanilla Nut Nog

2 1/2 cups brazil nuts
12 medjool dates, pitted
2 vanilla beans, or 1 tbsp vanilla extract
1/2 tsp ground cinnamon
water

1. Soak the brazil nuts in water to cover for 8 to 12 hours.
2. In a separate bowl, soak the dates and vanilla beans together in water to cover plus 2 inches, for 8 to 12 hours.
3. Drain the brazil nuts, rinse well, and drain again.
4. Remove dates and vanilla beans from the soaking water and add enough additional water to make 5 cups.
5. Pour into a blender, add the nuts and process until smooth.
6. Add the dates, cinnamon, and vanilla extract or vanilla beans to the blender. Blend again until smooth, stopping occasionally to scrape down the sides of the container.
7. Taste and add more dates, vanilla, water or cinnamon as desired, and process until smooth.
8. In small batches, pour blended mixture into a nut milk bag.* Gently squeeze out the liquid into a large bowl.
9. Pour the strained nog into clear cups, grate a bit of fresh nutmeg on top, and enjoy.

*A nut milk bag can be obtained from many sources online.

Courtesy of Nomi Shannon

Smoothies

Smoothies are a great way to get an abundance of high-quality vitamins, minerals, chlorophyll, fiber, essential fats, protein and energy for your muscles and brain. By contrast, most store-bought smoothies are loaded with sugar and dairy, and lack the valuable nutrients found in whole foods.

In the smoothie recipes that follow, not all the ingredients are mandatory. Feel free to branch out and be creative.

Green Goddess Smoothie

1 large handful parsley

3 to 4 chard leaves

2 stalks celery, cut into 1-inch pieces

1 cucumber, peeled, seeds removed, and cut into chunks

1 ripe banana

1/2 ripe avocado

1 1/2 cups fresh apple/celery/carrot juice

1 cup water

Optional: 1/2 lime or fresh ginger

**Place all ingredients in a high-powered blender and process
until very smooth.**

Courtesy of Diane Best

DELICIOUS, NUTRITIOUS AND SIMPLE

Green Delicious

    5 purple kale leaves
    1/4 avocado
    1 clove garlic
    juice of 1/2 lime
    2 cups water
    1/2 tsp salt
    2 roma tomatoes

Blend well in high-speed blender.

Courtesy of From Green For Life

Savory Smoothie

Yields 1 quart

    6 red leaf lettuce leaves
    1/4 bunch fresh basil
    1/2 lime, juiced
    1/2 red onion
    2 celery sticks
    1/4 avocado
    2 cups water

Blend well in high-speed blender.

Courtesy of From Green For Life

Holiday Dinner

Remember, festive celebrations can also be healthy! Enjoy this delicious, nutritious holiday meal.

MENU

Festive Salad with Pomegranate Seeds

Festive String Beans with Toasted Almonds

Veggie Turkey Roast

Mushroom Onion Gravy

Yam Orange Cups

Tofu Pumpkin Pie

Cashew Crème

Vanilla Nut Nog

Festive Salad with Pomegranate Seeds

1 head romaine lettuce, torn or chopped
1 small red onion, chopped
1 red bell pepper, chopped
1 cucumber, chopped
10 kalamata olives, pitted and sliced
12 cherry tomatoes, halved
1/2 cup pecans, chopped, toasted lightly in dry cast-iron fry pan
1/2 cup pomegranate seeds

Mix together ingredients and toss with Creamy Avocado Dressing (page 34).

Festive String Beans with Toasted Almonds

1 lb string beans with ends cut off
24 raw almonds, sliced or chopped coarsely
olive oil
1 tbsp tamari sauce
black pepper, freshly ground

1. Heat a cast iron fry pan to medium, add almonds and continuously stir until they turn a golden color. Remove and place in a cup.
2. Heat pan again and coat bottom thinly with oil.
3. Add string beans and coat with oil.
4. Stir in tamari sauce and add 1/4-inch of water, cover and simmer until beans are tender, but not soft. Remove from heat, add pepper and roll in toasted almonds.

DELICIOUS, NUTRITIOUS AND SIMPLE

Veggie Turkey Roast

8 oz whole cashew nuts

1/2 cup whole wheat breadcrumbs

1 egg, beaten

3 medium-sized parsnips, coarsely chopped

1 tsp fresh rosemary, or 1/2 tsp dried

1 tsp fresh thyme, or 1/2 tsp dried

pinch of sage

1 small onion, finely chopped

1 large clove garlic, crushed

1 tsp organic white or yellow miso paste

1/2 cup hot water

3 tbsp olive oil

8 oz mushrooms, chopped

Preheat oven to 350°F.

1. Grind cashews in a food processor or blender until fine and mix with breadcrumbs.
2. Add beaten egg to dry ingredients.
3. Sauté parsnips in 2 tbsp olive oil until soft, and then mash.
4. Mix parsnips and herbs into nut mixture.
5. In 1 tbsp olive oil, sauté onions with garlic until soft, and add to mixture.
6. Dissolve miso in 1/2 cup boiled water and add to mixture.
7. In 1 tbsp olive oil, sauté mushrooms, then add to mixture and mix all ingredients thoroughly.
8. Grease baking tray with olive oil and shape mixture into a turkey shape, or to make a loaf, put mixture into olive oil–greased pan.
9. Cover and bake in oven for 1 hour. Remove lid or foil and bake an additional 15 minutes uncovered.

Serve with Mushroom/Onion Gravy (page 122).

Mushroom/Onion Gravy

    2 tbsp olive oil
    1 small onion
    2 1/2 cups water
    2 tbsp cornstarch
    1 tsp tamari sauce
    1 tsp organic white or yellow miso paste
    1/2 tsp dried thyme
    1/2 tsp dried rosemary
    1/4 tsp dried sage
    1 bay leaf
    4 oz shitake mushrooms, sliced

1. Sauté onions in saucepan with 2 tbsp olive oil for 5 minutes.
2. Mix cornstarch with small amount of cold water (3 to 4 tbsp) to make a smooth white liquid.
3. Slowly add to sauce, stirring as you do so.
4. Add remaining ingredients.
5. Cover partially with lid and continue to stir occasionally until sauce thickens and cooks (20 minutes).

Yam/Orange Cups

    4 yams, medium-size
    4 oranges
    2 oz pecans, chopped
    8 whole pecans

Preheat oven to 350°F.

DELICIOUS, NUTRITIOUS AND SIMPLE

1. Bake yams 1 hour until tender.
2. Cut oranges in half and scoop out insides.
3. Place pulp in blender and blend slightly.
4. When yams are cooked, peel and place in mixing bowl.
5. Add pecans and 1 cup orange pulp and mash together.
6. Fill orange halves with mixture, forming a round cone on top.
7. With fork create circular texture, and top each yam with one whole pecan.
8. Place orange cups on baking tray and place under broiler a few minutes to reheat.

Tofu/Pumpkin Pie

1 1/2 packages tofu, extra-firm
2 cups pumpkin, cooked and puréed
2/3 cup honey
1 tsp vanilla
2 tsp cinnamon, ground
3/4 tsp ginger, ground
1/4 tsp nutmeg, ground
1/4 tsp cloves, ground

Preheat oven to 400°F.

1. Blend tofu in blender until smooth.
2. Add remaining ingredients and blend well.
3. Pour into Pie Crust (below) and bake for about 1 hour.
4. Chill and serve. Filling will be soft, but will firm up as it chills.

Pie Crust for Tofu/Pumpkin Pie

2 cups barley flour
1 cup oat flour

3 tbsp olive oil
1/2 to 3/4 cup water

1. Mix grains and add olive oil.
2. Add water to moisten. The dough should be as dry as possible to work with to ensure a softer crust.
3. Pre-bake the piecrust in a 9-inch pie dish for 5 minutes at 400°F, before filling with Tofu Pumpkin Pie mixture (page 123).

Cashew Crème

Way better than whipped cream! Smooth, sweet and rich.

1 cup cashews
4 medjool dates, pitted
1/2 small vanilla bean, or 1 tsp vanilla extract

1. Soak the cashews* in water to cover (plus 2 inches) for 8 to 12 hours.
2. In a separate bowl, soak the dates* and vanilla bean (if using) together in water to cover (plus 2 inches), for 8 to 12 hours.
3. Drain, rinse, and drain the cashews. Place cashews in a blender, add enough of the date-soaking water to barely cover them, and process until smooth and thick.
4. Add the dates (one at a time) plus vanilla, with enough date-soaking water to achieve a smooth, thick consistency, similar to whipped cream.

Variation: Macadamia nuts can be used in place of cashews.
*The cashews and dates must be soaked for the listed times for the ingredients to turn into whipped cream.

DELICIOUS, NUTRITIOUS AND SIMPLE

Vanilla Nut Nog

2 1/2 cups brazil nuts
12 medjool dates, pitted
2 vanilla beans, or 1 tbsp vanilla extract
1/2 tsp ground cinnamon
water

1. Soak the brazil nuts in water to cover for 8 to 12 hours.
2. In a separate bowl, soak the dates and vanilla beans together in water to cover plus 2 inches, for 8 to 12 hours.
3. Drain the brazil nuts, rinse well, and drain again.
4. Remove dates and vanilla beans from the soaking water and add enough additional water to make 5 cups.
5. Pour into a blender, add the nuts and process until smooth.
6. Add the dates, vanilla extract or vanilla beans, and cinnamon to the blender. Blend again until smooth, stopping occasionally to scrape down the sides of the container.
7. Taste and add more dates, vanilla, water or cinnamon as desired, and process until smooth.
8. In a fine strainer or nut milk bag* in a large bowl, pour the blended mixture into it in batches, and gently squeeze out the liquid. Pour the strained nog into clear cups, grate a bit of fresh nutmeg on top, and enjoy.

*A nut milk bag can be obtained from many sources on the web.

Courtesy of Nomi Shannon

Cleansing Recipes

Cleansing recipes are basically high nutrients in very simple-to-digest food or drink. Because these are metabolized so quickly and easily, energy is freed up to be more available for the body to use where most needed.

When one is experiencing symptoms, whether of a cold, flu, or intestinal upset, a few meals of cleansing recipes usually help the body to resolve the challenge sooner. Even when one isn't challenged, especially in warm weather, doing a one- to three-day cleanse (meaning only cleansing foods) gives the body the opportunity to flush out any build-up of excess waste and do extra refinement and balance.

It is important when cleansing to rest and keep warm, so that energy isn't pulled to the surface muscles and diluted, and is therefore more available to the inside processes. If the body is rejecting food, as in cases of nausea or intestinal upset, it may be best just to rest and drink only purified water, even for a whole day.

Kidney Flush Drink

This drink is cleansing and healing for the kidneys and bladder, and helps to quickly flush waste out of the body.

1 lemon, peeled and seeded
cayenne pepper, powder
1 tbsp pure maple syrup (Grade B)

In a blender, liquefy the lemon in 2 oz water. Then add 3 shakes of cayenne pepper, 14 oz water, and the maple syrup, and blend again.

Juice Fast

Make an 8- to 10-ounce glass of fresh juice every three hours throughout the day.

1. First juice: 2 medium carrots, 3 celery stalks, 1 kale leaf.
2. Three hours later, have second juice: 1 tomato, 1 whole cucumber, handful of parsley.
3. Three hours later, have third fresh juice: 3 apples or 3 pears, or enough grapes to make 8 to 10 oz.
4. Three hours later, go back to first juice and repeat the same juices throughout the day.

Watermelon Fast

During the summer when it is warm and organic watermelons are available, this is a delicious and easy cleanse. Eat one bowlful of cut-up watermelon every three hours throughout the day.

DELICIOUS, NUTRITIOUS AND SIMPLE

Cilantro Chelation Pesto

Two teaspoons of this cilantro pesto daily for three weeks is purportedly enough to increase the urinary excretion of mercury, lead, and aluminum, thus effectively removing these toxic metals from our bodies. Consider doing this cleanse for 3 weeks at least once a year.

4 cloves garlic

1/3 cup brazil nuts (selenium source)

1/3 cup sunflower seeds (cysteine source)

1/3 cup pumpkin seeds (zinc/magnesium sources)

2 cups packed fresh cilantro (vitamin A source)

2/3 cup flaxseed oil (important to be from a dark glass bottle, refrigerated)

4 tbsp lemon juice (vitamin C source)

2 tsp dulse powder

tamari sauce

1. Process cilantro and flaxseed oil in a blender until cilantro is chopped.
2. Add garlic, nuts, seeds, dulse, and lemon juice and blend until mixture forms a fine paste.
3. Add a squirt of tamari sauce to taste and blend again.
4. Store refrigerated in dark glass jar.

Creamy Blended Soup

1 carrot	2 chard leaves
1 zucchini	2 tbsp parsley, finely chopped
1 onion	

Optional: Chinese cabbage, butternut squash, string beans, bok choy

1. Cut up all vegetables and place in pot.
2. Fill water to barely cover vegetables.
3. Cover with lid and bring to a boil, then reduce heat to a simmer.
4. Cook 10 minutes.
5. Place mixture in blender or use a hand-held immersion blender, and blend into a creamy soup.

Simple Miso Soup

2 heaping tbsp organic white or yellow miso paste

1 scallion, chopped

1 small carrot, finely sliced

2 shitake mushrooms

4 cups water

1 tsp dried wakame seaweed (only from Maine), soaked for 1 minute and rinsed

1. Bring water to a boil and add all the veggies, cover and simmer for 10 minutes.
2. Turn off heat, let sit for 5 minutes, then remove 1 cup of liquid and place in a cup with miso. Stir until miso is dissolved, and pour back into soup and mix together.

Helpful Hints

Organic Produce

When possible, it is wise to use fresh, local, organic, non-GMO produce, especially from farmers markets. These fresh foods contain higher amounts of nutrients than non-organic foods (sometimes twice as much). They also are free of toxic pesticides that the body needs to defend against and attempt to excrete.

Food Combining

If you have sensitive digestion, it is wise to choose simple food combinations. Otherwise basic common sense and experimentation will guide you. I do suggest, along with salads, vegetables and fruit, to choose only one complex food per meal, rich in either complex carbohydrates (grains, beans, potatoes, yams) or concentrated proteins (nuts, seeds, beans, soy, animal products). This helps conserve energy output and digestive time.

GMOs

Testing has shown that long-term effects of GMOs are troublesome—that GMO foods have created disease in many lab animals, especially cancer. Many countries around the world have banned GMO crops.

It appears that GMOs (genetically modified organisms) are more widely used in this country than previously known. In fact, most vegetables are probably genetically modified, unless specifically indicated on food labels otherwise. This is especially true for corn and soy products. Since labeling of GMO foods is not yet mandatory, we should look for a non-GMO label, even on organic foods, since we cannot assume all organic products are non-GMOs.

Veggie Prep (quick, easy & fresh!)

Juicing and making salads can be a lot of work, and keeping the veggies fresh can be a problem. However, there is a way to make it quick and easy and have veggies stay fresh for up to a week.

After you buy your vegetables, clean them right away. Cut the ends off the celery, carrots, and other vegetables, scrub with a veggie brush, and soak greens in filtered water. Let all drip-dry for about 10 minutes in a colander and then store in large airtight, rectangular food storage containers in the fridge. You should have one container for juicing veggies and one for salad veggies. After that, when you want to make a juice, you just whip out the container and it takes 3 minutes to juice and 5 minutes to clean the juicer, and you're good to go.

Likewise, it takes just a few minutes to make a salad, once everything is washed. Best of all, the greens stay puffed up and fresher longer after being washed. Go for it!

Juicers

Juicers that get the most nutrients from vegetables are called Slow Speed Juicers or Mastication Juicers. They operate at low speeds of 80 RPM and use an auger that presses the vegetables rather than rather than ripping them apart. In this way they are more like a wine press (which crushes juice from grapes) than like a blender or food processor. They are able to effectively juice barley grass, parsley and leafy greens as well as all other vegetables and fruit. These types of juicers are also multifunctional. They can make ice cream out of frozen fruit and butters out of nuts. On top of all of this, they are easy to clean. (Well, not with the nut butters, but with the juicing!) Make your juicer your most used appliance.

Soy

Soy has several pros and cons. The cons are that it can cause indigestion in some individuals, inhibit digestive enzymes, and slow down the thyroid in those with borderline hypothyroidism. The pros are that it is concentrated protein, and it may have a helpful influence on hormonal imbalances. Additionally, it has a fairly healthy record, as it has been around for a very long time (especially in the East), though usually consumed in smaller quantities than in the modern diet.

When fermented, as in miso, tempeh, and nama shoyu sauce, most of the problematic issues are eliminated. When using any form of soy, it is wise to get organic non-GMO soy, as the non-organic soy is a very pesticide-laden crop. When using tamari, I suggest getting organic, wheat-free, unpasteurized nama shoyu sauce.

Refined Carbohydrates

It is best to avoid refined carbohydrates such as white flour and sugar, high-fructose corn syrup, breads and pasta. Besides usually being low in nutrients, their concentrated calories create a sugar spike in the blood. This puts a strain on the pancreas to produce more insulin, and can lead to diabetes. Additionally, much of the refined carbs convert to stored fat in the body.

Cleaning Non-Organic Produce

If you use non-organic produce, soak vegetables and fruit for 5 minutes in a large bowl of cold water with 2 tbsp of white vinegar, then scrub with a vegetable brush. Non-organic fruit should be peeled, if possible.

Cooking Vegetables

Steaming or pressure-cooking retains more nutrients than most other forms of cooking. When steaming vegetables, use filtered water. Some of the vitamins and minerals leach into this water, which can be used in soups or drinks to recapture these nutrients.

Clean Water

Most of us know that pure filtered water, free of chlorine, fluoride, and other contaminants, is the best choice for cooking and drinking. Yet there are hidden problems in the storage of filtered water. The reverse osmosis system creates very pure water, but unfortunately it is usually stored in metal containers lined with polypropylene. Water sitting in plastic bottles leaches out some of the plastic polymers. There are excellent water filters that filter water from the faucet through the filter and then out again with no storage. These appear to be among the best choices for clean water.

Of all the purified water, distilled water is the purest with the least amount of contaminants. However, there is much controversy over whether or not it leaches minerals out of the body or whether it is too acidic, since it does not contain the alkaline minerals. In the end, I have never seen or read any legitimate testing to prove these theories. If one does choose distilled water, make sure it is only stored in glass.

As for water on-the-go, fill up a stainless steel or glass bottle at home to ensure you have clean drinking water throughout the day.

Ultimately, the healthiest water is the water from food, i.e., fruits and veggies. It is naturally structured and charged with life energy, and forms beautiful crystals when frozen, unlike purified or filtered water. Eating fruit or juicing fresh vegetables (and drinking the juice immediately) are by far two of the healthiest ways to consume water.

Eggs

The healthiest, most wholesome eggs are from chickens that are raised free-range, hormone-free, and fed a vegetarian, non-GMO diet, as is the case in the farmyard, except for an occasional bug or worm. An extra nutritional plus is added if the eggs are fertile.

Fish

The healthiest fish to consume are wild fish, not farmed, as farmed fish usually do not contain the healthy omega-3 oils. This is because farmed fish often do not have the same exercise challenges or eat the natural foods of the sea. Farmed fish may also contain residues of drugs given to fight disease in crowded fish farms. Some farmed fish are fed dog food or other products that are unnatural for fish to eat. Furthermore, many farmed fish are now being genetically modified, another potentially dangerous and threateningly short-sighted science breakthrough.

Large fish, such as tuna, shark and swordfish, usually contain higher amounts of mercury since they are at the top of the food chain, therefore less consumption of these is probably wise. And since the nuclear accident at Fukushima, an unimaginable amount of radioactive waste continues to flood the Pacific Ocean, with no end in sight. How this affects the fish we eat is not forthcoming in the news, as it risks damaging a huge industry. Since there is a fair amount of controversy over the radiation concerns of Pacific Ocean fish, it may be wise to be cautious about fish choices along with any seaweed products produced in Japan.

Poultry or Meat

When buying poultry or meat, organically raised, free-range, hormone-free, and grass-fed (for beef) are the healthiest choices. They also create the least suffering for the animals.

Dairy

Cow's milk contains a large casein molecule that is meant to help a calf gain 1,000 lbs in one year. It may be too large for most humans, as milk has created digestive problems, allergies, mucus overproduction, and even reactive dairy antibodies in large segments of the population.

Even Dr. Spock, from the 1960s, felt no child should drink cow milk before the age of two because it somehow could contribute to childhood diabetes. Therefore I don't suggest people consume this product.

Goat and sheep milk products seem to be different. Perhaps it is because they are closer in size to humans and the protein molecules and composition are closer to the structure of human milk. Many people who are allergic to cow milk can drink goat milk without any ill effect.

Furthermore, many cow milk products contain growth hormones, which are suspected of contributing to extra estrogen in the body. This may be the cause of the recent phenomenon of young girls reaching puberty younger than ever before—at eight or nine—and the vast increase in hormone-related cancer in both men and women.

Wheat

Wheat has been hybridized to the degree that it appears different from what it once was 100 years ago, and now contains a kind of gluten protein that many, many people are allergic to. Some even develop a digestive disease called celiac disease. Therefore, it is wise to avoid wheat or keep it as an occasional food. It can be replaced with other whole grains that do not contain gluten, such as brown rice, corn, amaranth, millet, quinoa, sorghum, and teff.

Healthiest Oils and Fats

The safest oil to use is cold-pressed or extra-virgin olive oil in dark glass: it is tried and true! It can be stored in a cool dark cupboard. Occasionally, small amounts of toasted sesame oil are fine for seaweed and oriental salads.

Avoid hydrogenated oils and margarine, as they contain trans-fatty acids that have been proven to be potentially harmful to cells. They are foreign to the body, and can create functional problems that undermine the health of the organs.

For light grilling in a cast-iron frying pan, or coating baking pans, use olive oil, organic ghee or organic coconut oil (from a glass container). Cook only on low/medium so that the oil does not reach "smoking" temperature. When sautéing vegetables, add a little water or broth to the pan after a minute, as this ensures the oils are not overheated.

Avoid canola oil, as its fumes have caused breast cancer in animals in lab tests.

More and more studies are confirming that good quantities of healthy omega-3 fats in our food seem to promote healing of many inflammatory diseases such as arthritis, heart disease, and even cancer. The best sources of omega-3 fats are nuts and seeds (especially flax, chia and hemp seeds), avocados and olives. These fats are also concentrated in coldwater fish. If the nuts or seeds are roasted and heated above 110°F, the omega-3 oils are destroyed.

Adding oil-rich foods like avocado or nuts to salads helps to absorb the vitamins of the carotene family found in many red, orange, and green foods. It is also important that seeds are not previously ground up—as in many protein shake mixes—since the fragile omega-3 oils become rancid very quickly when exposed to oxygen, light or heat. If grinding is needed, it is best to do within 5 minutes of consuming the ground-up seeds.

Healthiest Cookware

Pots and pans made from glass*, stainless steel, enamel (that is not scratched), and cast-iron are the safest, healthwise, to use. Aluminium and coated non-stick pans should be avoided as they may leach traces of toxic chemicals into food.

Glass cooking pots, called Visionware, are no longer being produced, but are available on eBay and from thrift stores.

Food Labels and Additives

Limit the use of processed, packaged foods as they are usually loaded with many chemical additives. More importantly, read the ingredients! Many foods that advertise a healthier choice contain hidden sugars and chemicals. If you read an ingredient you've never heard of before, chances are it is a chemical additive or a hidden form of sugar.

Avoid foods with chemical preservatives, flavorings, and added food colorings, especially sodium benzoate, which is used as a preservative in soda and candies. It is banned in European countries and is associated with hyperactive behavior. The same is true with most sugar substitutes.

Also avoid food with the thickener carrageen in it. Even though it is originally from seaweed, lab tests suggest it may have a cancer-causing aspect to it.

Compost

It is so easy to compost your fruits and vegetable scraps. It makes great fertilizer for your plants, and it decreases waste and creates a healthier earth.

Nutrition & the Healing Process

AN IMPORTANT NOTE

When you start to consume high amounts of nutrient-dense foods, profound changes can happen. Not only will your cells have more than enough nutrients to get through the day, they will have extra raw materials available to them that can be used for deeper healing. Areas of the body challenged by sluggishness, toxicity, stored waste, and degeneration or diseased tissue will be more potently cleansed, repaired and regenerated. This occurs most intensely at night when we are sleeping, since less energy is being used by muscle and digestive activity.

Depending on the depth and severity of your challenges, you may feel tired and weak for short periods of time as the body's energy becomes directed inwards to focus on healing work. You may occasionally experience different "detox" symptoms, such as loose stools, headaches, rashes, fever, blemishes, aches and pains, inflammation, phlegm, and other discharges. Sometimes, if deep extensive healing is needed, these remedial actions can go on for a few days or longer.

This is a normal response. I encourage you to pay close attention to what is going on. During these times, your body will usually give a loud, clear message to rest, both energetically and digestively. This means you need to conserve your energy by taking naps, refraining from exercise, and even requiring more extended bed rest at times.

Digestive rest means eating only easy-to-digest foods that do not demand a lot of time and energy to be broken down and absorbed.

Good foods that conserve energy and allow the digestive tract to rest while still maintaining high-nutrient levels include freshly made vegetable juices, blended vegetable soups, steamed vegetables, fruit, soft-boiled eggs, and plentiful water and herbal teas.

If you experience more intense symptoms, such as a mild fever or nausea, I suggest fasting on only water or freshly made vegetable juices every three hours for a day or two (see Juice Cleansing Recipes, page 126). During this time patience is rewarded, for if the body is allowed to complete this process without interference, afterwards you will usually experience greater energy, mental clarity, and balance. Old health issues may be lessened or cleared up entirely.

There are additional ways to help alleviate symptoms so that you do not suppress the cleansing and healing process, but instead help them resolve. These include acupuncture, massage, restorative yoga, and colon hydrotherapy. All of these modalities stimulate the circulation of blood and lymphatic fluid, speed up the process of cleansing and healing, and make the experience more comfortable. If you are concerned that your symptoms are more serious, I encourage you to seek the support of a healthcare practitioner familiar with the detoxification and healing process.

Travel Healthy

My clients constantly ask how they can best eat healthy while traveling, since this can be a big challenge.

If traveling by car, I suggest bringing an ice chest with raw vegetable sticks (made from carrots, cucumbers, celery, jicama, and bell peppers), cherry tomatoes, radishes, and apples — plus dips like guacamole and hummus or nut butters. Adding fruit, nuts, hard-boiled eggs, avocado, cooked baby potatoes, and popcorn make filling healthy snacks as well as simple meals, especially if no suitable restaurant is available.

When I travel by car long distances, I usually bring a hot plate, a pot, rolled oats or chia and hemp seeds, plus my juicer and cleaned veggies. I make vegetable juice and porridge in the motel room for a great start to the day.

As far as eating at restaurants on the road is concerned, if I carefully scan the menu I usually find one or two things I can choose that are reasonably wholesome, like baked potatoes or beans.

For special vacations, where food is part of the delight or adventure, I suggest having two reasonably clean, simple meals, and then indulge a little on the third meal each day. For example, enjoy a dessert, glass of wine, or other special treat. This helps maintain good energy, good digestive function, and good nutrient levels.

For long-distance plane rides, taking half-a-dozen cooked baby potatoes, and an avocado to spread on each half, is delicious and easy. Adding vegetable sticks, hard-boiled eggs, or fruit and nuts helps to get through travel time and arrive feeling good.

When I'm in a new city or foreign country, I always call health food stores to get information from locals in the know about where to go for delicious, nutritious food at nearby restaurants and juice bars. From the Champs-Élysees in Paris to Istikial Street in Istanbul, there are great places to eat that will also support your health and well-being.

INDEX by Sections

DELICIOUS, NUTRITIOUS AND SIMPLE

INDEX Alphabetical

DELICIOUS, NUTRITIOUS AND SIMPLE

Biography

Dale Figtree, Ph.D., is a Nutritional Health Practitioner with a private nutritional counseling practice in Santa Barbara, California. She is the author of *Beyond Cancer Treatment: Clearing and Healing the Underlying Causes*, and *Eat Smart, Feel Great!*, plus the video/DVD *The Joy of Nutrition*. Dr. Figtree has taught western nutrition at the Santa Barbara College of Oriental Medicine, and continues to give seminars and talks throughout the United States and Europe.

Made in the USA
San Bernardino, CA
04 May 2018